how to start a home-based

Housecleaning Business third edition

Laura Jorstad and Melinda Morse

gpp®

Guilford, Connecticut

Copyright © 2002, 2005, 2009 Morris Book Publishing, LLC

Morse, Melinda.
How to start a home-based housecleaning business / by Laura Jorstad and Melinda Morse. – 3rd ed.
          p. cm. – (Home-based business series)
Includes index.
ISBN 0-7627-5014-6
1. Building cleaning industry — United States — Management. 2. Home-based businesses — United States — Management. 3. New Business enterprises — United States — Management. 4. Small Business — United States — Management. 5. House cleaning — United States — Management. I. Title: Housecleaning business. II. Jorstad, Laura. III. Title IV. Series.

HD9999.B883 U655 2002
648'.5'0681—dc21   2002072679

Printed in the United States of America
10 9 8 7 6 5 4 3 2 1

Contents

Acknowledgments

Thanks to all the great folks at The Globe Pequot Press, especially Keith Wallman. Special thanks to all the cleaners who so generously let me pick their brains for advice, suggestions, complaints, and laughter: Phil and Sandy Adams of Domestic Goddess; David and Mary of Experience Green; Michael and Jessica of GreenSweep; Deanna Hains of Zen Home Cleaning; Barb Brown in Vermont; Linda in Minneapolis. All my love and thanks to Dad and Ruth; Eric, Sherlyn, and the menagerie; my niece Krista, my niece Jessie, and my other niece Jessy; and to Mom. Plus mega gratitude to and for the publishing industry as a whole. In my world, books are life, and I've yet to meet one single book professional who didn't agree wholeheartedly. What a great way to make a living.
—L. J.

I wish to thank Byron Reese of PageWise Inc. for not hitting the delete button. A special thanks to small-business consultant Lisa Solari-Parravicini, and many thanks to Mary Norris of The Globe Pequot Press.
—M. M.

Introduction: Why a Home-Based Business?

The twenty-first century has been challenging for all of us. The only certainty about the world, it seems, is that it's uncertain.

The insecurity reaches straight down to our work—what we do for most of our waking hours to contribute to the world, and to support the folks we love. Jobs are tenuous. Companies are tenuous. Whole *industries* are seeing upheaval.

So why a home-based business? Isn't the world scary enough without putting our money, time, and integrity on the line? Well, one cleaning-services entrepreneur said of founding his own business: "It's allowed me to control my own destiny—my own schedule—my own lifestyle. I don't have to wait for a paycheck. I can make money every day, even every night, as long as I'm willing to do the work."

This is the twenty-first-century American Dream—to create our own success, on our own terms. If that means taking a risk, it's worth it for the chance to take ownership of our own lives. Think about it: Who do you trust more than yourself and the folks right there under your roof? You don't have to wait for independence if you're an entrepreneur. You just take it.

What is an entrepreneur? What does it take to be an entrepreneur? The term refers to anyone who launches or manages a business venture, often assuming risks. It's nothing new—it's been around as long as human history. Hyman Lipman, who in 1858 came up with the idea of placing rubber erasers on the ends of pencils, made $100,000 from the sale of the patent alone! Mary Kay Ash founded Mary Kay Cosmetics in 1963 with a $5,000 investment and turned it into a $2 billion company. And half a century before Mary Kay came Madam C. J. Walker, born Sarah Breedlove. The daughter of former slaves on a Louisiana plantation, this turn-of-the-twentieth-century washerwoman used $1.50—then a week's wages—to make the first batch of Wonderful Hair Grower, which she sold door-to-door. Her personal fortune at her time of death totaled some $2 million.

These folks and millions like them began right where they lived, at home. It's where the heart is, sure—but it's also where the heating bills are already being paid. And the rent or mortgage. Not much traffic or road rage on the way to work. Among people desperate for income but short on capital, working from home makes sense.

Some of the best home-based businesses include adventure tourism, bed-and-breakfasts, catering, event planning, interior design, landscaping, and consulting work of all kinds, from weddings to software. Not to mention housecleaning! There's no limit to the possibilities for those who are creative, resourceful, and able to seize opportunities. Most of the people who start home-based businesses are able to earn at least an extra income. Some entrepreneurs have been able to turn their endeavors into very profitable full-time careers.

Not long ago the term *small business* brought to mind a little mom-and-pop corner store, or a one-person home-improvement provider who did the landscaping, the painting, and everything in between. Home-based workers were looked on with pity for failing to obtain real jobs. No more. Home-based entrepreneurs are now role models.

Family, friends, and neighbors seeking to do the same often approach these workers for advice. Small businesses are dynamic job creators, offering real opportunity for many who in the past had little access to economic power, as well as for those who want to take control of their own futures.

Indeed, small businesses may be the key to the economy of the United States, generating new opportunities for growth, which in turn creates new employment opportunities for diverse and underrepresented groups. Small businesses also help establish new products and innovative services in the current and future marketplace.

If the events of the twenty-first century have taught us anything, it is that things can change . . . fast. And in a world where what's here today could be gone in a heartbeat, there's a kind of security that comes from being self-sufficient.

As an entrepreneur, you are in charge of your career and your life—not your boss, not company management, but you. You decide when and how much to work. You decide what fees to charge. When you work for yourself, no one can take your job away from you—ever. If things change in your life or your world, you can adapt your business right along with them. It's a different kind of safety net than you'll have at a corporate job, a kind that makes sense in the new millennium.

If you've ever considered starting a home-based business, now is the time to do it!

Considering a Home-Based Housecleaning Business

If you're holding this book, put aside everything you have ever read or heard about starting a home-based business. For now, forget about investments, start-up costs, loans, and taxes. And especially forget about fancy vacations on cruise ships and impressing the neighbors with the latest-model SUV.

Starting a Business: The Reality

You've probably heard the fantasies sold by business start-up classes, seminars, Web sites, and infomercials: Starting a business requires only a few hours a day, and it is so easy. So easy that anyone can do it, and once you learn the secrets, you can instantaneously generate so much profit that within months, you'll be able to pay off your mortgage in full and travel around the world.

Here's the reality: Mass-marketed business start-up schemes conceal the three most basic components of any home-business ownership:

- Businesses are built, not created out of thin air.
- Business owners work harder for themselves than they ever did for anyone else.
- The single most important investment that you will make is in yourself.

Unless you've inherited a successful business, which is unlikely if you're reading this book, the first guiding principle is that all businesses are built from the ground up. To think otherwise is known in the business world as magical thinking, or the Lucky Charm illusion.

You cannot buy formulas or secrets. Building a business requires more energy, stamina, commitment, and desire to get it right than does working for someone else or for someone else's corporation. If working for yourself appeals to you, be prepared to work harder for yourself than you ever have for anyone else.

Many first-time business owners spend their life savings on advertising, equipment, services, and other products but soon go out of business because they never realized the truth about investing: The most important investment that you will ever make is in yourself.

Home-business start-ups end up in one of three ways:

1. They never get past the pondering or planning stage.
2. They fail because the business was not built from the bottom up. Too many beginning small-business owners will envision a five-story mansion and start to build the first floor. Somewhere around the stairs to the second floor, though, things begin to crumble. The owners forgot, ignored, or simply didn't know that they needed to lay a foundation before attempting to build from the ground up.
3. They succeed.

How do you make sure your business succeeds? You lay a foundation. The foundation is the plan behind why you are doing what you are doing, as well as a plan for where you are going. Without the foundation, you don't have a business.

If research, marketing, and physically working are not your cup of tea, then a home-based cleaning business isn't for you. Owning and operating a home-based business is no less work than any other professional career, whether as an attorney, a doctor, an accountant, or a plumber. It's not easy money. It's not a get-rich-quick plot or a path to overnight success. Any successful home business is a progressive operation with an ongoing plan for working, improving the work, and profiting from that work.

A home-based *cleaning* firm may be even more labor-intensive than other home businesses. To a woman—and man—the cleaners we talked to for this third edition pointed to the need for a tireless work ethic. Asked about the hardest part of the job, one cleaner said, "Doing the work! This is not an easy job." Another noted, "You have to clean all day, then go home and work on the administrative functions as well. And you have no choice but to stay at the computer until it's done." Cleaning well is hard physical work, and growing a business is hard emotionally, spiritually, and intellectually.

That's the reality. But here's another truth: Becoming self-employed could be the best thing you'll ever do for yourself. Owning your own business can enable you

What About Franchising?

The Molly Maid cleaning company was founded in Canada in 1979 and has now completed more than twelve million individual cleanings. There are branches in forty U.S. states and several other countries. Pairs of fully trained Molly Maid personnel complete each cleaning assignment; all are uniformed, insured, and bonded.

Molly Maid's basic home service includes dusting, floor cleaning, and vacuuming. Cabinet fronts and hardware are wiped, and kitchen and bathroom fixtures are cleaned. On special request, the company offers custom services such as oven, refrigerator, and carpet cleaning.

Molly Maid is only one example of a cleaning-service provider that uses the franchise model of operation. You've heard of this model—these days, it's hard to miss such franchising businesses as McDonald's, Baskin-Robbins, and 7-Eleven. But these familiar firms are far from the only franchisors out there. Many, many other product and service companies are joining them on the franchise wagon, including, of course, cleaning-service providers.

So what is the franchise model? For an initial investment (which ranges from five to six figures, depending on the company and type of business), franchisees are provided with all the information, training, and materials they need to start up a branch of the business serving a particular territory. You own the franchise, but you're also obligated to follow guidelines set forth by the parent company.

Cleaning-service franchisors generally require an initial investment of anywhere from $36,000 to $135,000. As the franchise owner, you won't be cleaning any homes yourself; instead, you'll be recruiting, training, and managing a staff of employees who provide the elbow grease.

There are many other housecleaning franchise operators out there, each with its own required investment, benefits and drawbacks, and level of support. Given the risk that franchising entails, you'll want to investigate all these opportunities very carefully. And remember that the franchising company wants you to make money, but it also expects to turn a profit itself! Nevertheless, for the right person, franchising may be an option worth investigating—either now or for your future.

Benefits of Franchising

- You're provided with a known and respected company name; a territory; and established procedures for all phases of doing business (from the cleaning itself right down to the purchasing, billing, and record keeping).

- Equipment and materials come with your investment.

- You're provided with computer software to run your business (as well as technical support for running the software).

- You have a network of peers—folks doing the exact same work you're doing, in other parts of the country or the world—who are not your competitors. They're on your side. They're ready to offer help, advice, and/or shoulders to cry on.

- Marketing and advertising materials are already prepared for you. Some franchisors will even sign up your customers for you.

Drawbacks of Franchising

- Money. All of the benefits listed above must be paid for. Opening a franchise requires an initial investment that can run well into six figures.

- Then there are all the ongoing business expenses you're responsible for in any venture (and franchising is no exception): supplies (from glass cleaner to Post-it notes); equipment (vacuum cleaners, photocopy machines, company automobiles, and the like); services (lawyers, accountants, and repair folks, among others); and so on.

- Franchisors may also charge royalty fees and marketing fees on an ongoing basis.

- Some franchisors require you to purchase supplies from them. They may also require you to own and maintain vehicles for all your staff.

Cleaning Franchisors

Here are a few of the cleaning franchise networks you may wish to research:

- Molly Maid, www.mollymaid.com

- CottageCare, www.cottagecare.com

- The Green Mop, an eco-friendly cleaning company, is (as this book goes to press) working toward offering franchise opportunities. If you're interested in green cleaning, visit www.greenmopfranchise.com for the latest info.

- Maid Brigade, www.maidbrigadefranchise.com

- MaidPro, www.maidpro.com

- Maid to Perfection, www.maidtoperfectioncorp.com

- Merry Maids, www.merrymaids.com

Franchise Resources

If you'd like more information on franchising in general, or on specific franchise opportunities in the housecleaning arena (or just about any other arena conceivable), here are some resources to get you started:

- Bison, the franchise network, www.bison.com

- International Franchise Association, www.franchise.org

- FRANdata, www.frandata.com

- Franchise.com, www.franchise.com

- Franchise Zone, part of *Entrepreneur* magazine, www.entrepreneur.com/franzone

- Franchise Advantage, www.franchiseadvantage.com

- *Franchising for Dummies* by Dave Thomas and Michael Seid

- *Franchising 101: The Complete Guide to Evaluating, Buying, and Growing Your Franchise Business* by the Association of Small Business Development Centers, edited by Ann Dugan

- *Franchise Update* magazine, www.franchise-update.com

- *Franchise Times* magazine, www.franchisetimes.com

This list is just the tip of the iceberg. For more resources than you can possibly manage, simply type "franchise" into a search engine and go to it.

Another hint: You may want to explore the idea of working for a cleaning-services franchise before branching out on your own. It's not for everyone, but it can offer you an inside look at what a housecleaner's job is like, as well as an opportunity to gather references who can vouch for your good work.

to enjoy the pride, self-esteem, and sense of accomplishment that go along with having created something fulfilling that works for you and that reflects your hard work and dedication. Not a lot of folks can say that about their careers. Just ask Joe there—the one in the thirty-seventh cubicle on the left.

Melinda's Story

When I started my housecleaning business, I had about $80 in the bank. Everything else I learned and earned. The biggest investment that I made was in myself.

My background of abandoned career paths isn't much different from anyone else's story. As is the case with most people who are looking for job opportunities, or who are changing careers, the why comes before the how. I didn't start my home-based cleaning business with any sort of business knowledge. I never even intended to start a business. I couldn't find a job to help me work my way through college, so I set out to create one. I thought it would be a temporary fix, something to pay bills until I was out of school. Yet I managed to build and establish a successful home-based cleaning business that I am proud to say I created, I built, I own, and I benefit from. Four years after founding my business, I was a successful entrepreneur and CEO with much more than $80 in the bank.

When I graduated from high school, I had no idea what I wanted to do. I knew what I needed to do, and that was work. I never thought about employee benefits, investments, promotions, or job security. I started what I now call the "job habit." I worked to maintain: to pay the rent, the car insurance, the utilities. There was never any money left over for vacations, savings, or those little fringe benefits like matching forks and spoons. Over the years I hopped from job to job in the hope of encountering the Shangri-la that I'd heard so much about: a career with a corporation that would pay me enough money to have matching forks and spoons, and one that would also pay for my funeral. I didn't find it. Instead I was, like most people, one paycheck away from financial devastation, and I didn't think I had any marketable skills. I certainly didn't have $25,000 stashed away to invest in a business.

The idea of a career finally occurred to me in my late twenties. In 1994 I decided to pursue my love for literature and hauled myself off to college. My plan was to become an English teacher. Reading and writing were my first loves, and I thought that by teaching English, I would be able to read and write to my heart's content while at the same time turning on America's youth to the wonderful world of literature.

But I still needed to make ends meet while pursuing my plan. And finding part-time employment to correspond with my part-time class load was difficult. Moreover, my sort of enthusiasm was meaningless to employers who were looking for people to answer telephones or to punch keys on a cash register. The jobs I'd relied on as a younger person—salesclerk, temporary office administrative assignments, and a variety of entry-level positions at various companies—were no longer an option for me. Nobody said *You're too old,* but they didn't hire me.

I needed to find work, and fast.

One afternoon at the post office, where I had just dumped off a pile of résumés that surely went into more than one round file, I ran into Ms. Weathers, the mother of a childhood acquaintance. I hadn't seen her in more than ten years. When she asked, "How are you?" I answered, "Not so good."

To my surprise, Ms. Weathers didn't just skip over my comment. She stopped and listened to me with heartfelt respect as I complained about the lack of part-time opportunities; about employers not returning phone calls or responding to résumés; about lying awake worrying that my car would be repossessed in the middle of the night. Then she told me she knew how I felt, because she'd been in my shoes. Ms. Weathers said in a proud voice, "That's why I clean houses." Over a good, long cup of coffee, she explained her plan.

Ms. Weathers had been a single mom for close to fifteen years. Her husband had died, leaving her without any savings or insurance benefits. There was a huge mortgage on the house, and she had no work experience other than a typing job she'd had as a teenager in the early 1960s. Yet she managed to put two children through college, keep on top of her mortgage, and still have money left for a car, a dog, and vacations twice a year.

I listened to her story, and felt a bit guilty for complaining about my so-called down-and-out life. Then Ms. Weathers suggested that I try to pick up a few house-cleaning jobs, "just until you get on your feet." I told her that I'd think about it, even though I never thought I would.

Housecleaning? Me? No thanks. I knew nothing about how to clean a house. In my own apartment, if paper towels and whatever bottle of spray cleaner was on sale that week didn't work, then whatever the stain was, it was going to stay there.

But later that evening I thought about Ms. Weathers. Somehow she was making it, and she had been for more than fifteen years. Perhaps it might be something I could do for a few months to catch up on the bills. I thought, *Well, how hard can it be?* I told myself I'd just follow the instructions on the backs of the cleaning-fluid bottles. I came up with scenarios in my head. I'd find elderly people who wanted a housecleaner because they were lonely and wouldn't notice or care if I missed a spot. Or I'd find a few rich bachelors who traveled all the time and just wanted their furniture lightly dusted. Perhaps I'd find people who were handicapped and couldn't reach the tops of cabinets to dust them off.

I had a lot to learn.

And I did learn it—all too often the hard way. That's what this book is for. As you think about, make plans for, and then start up your own home-based housecleaning business, I hope my own experiences and hard-won knowledge can help you out. Maybe there are a few lessons you won't have to learn the hard way.

Let's get started.

Is a Home-Based Housecleaning Business Right for You?

There's one critical requirement if you're going to pursue a housecleaning business: You have to be in reasonably good health. This is a physical job; you'll be on your feet most of the day, bending, stooping, reaching, moving in sometimes unusual ways, and lifting occasionally heavy weights (and lots of light ones). It can add up to aches and pains by the end of the day for anyone, no matter what kind of shape you're in. That's why you need to take a realistic look at the state of your health and the kinds of physical demands you'll be facing before you begin. If you have chronic health issues that limit your ability to do certain things, you might need to reconsider your plans.

What else should you think about? As with any career, the more skills and talents you bring to your business, the better off you'll be. But one of the joys of owning your own business is that you can build it around your strengths and interests. If you're someone who thrives on routine, for instance, you might want to focus on finding a few good regular clients. If you like lots of variety, on the other hand, perhaps you can network with a caterer or party planner and focus on cleaning before or after special occasions.

What else should you think about? First of all, here are some things you *don't* have to be to thrive in a housecleaning career:

- **You don't have to be a great housekeeper yourself.** Sure, if your own home is a mess, your friends and family might tease you about it. The truth is, however, there is a difference between cleaning to suit yourself and cleaning to meet other people's needs. If you have a sense of professionalism—a strong desire to give your clients excellent service—you should do fine.
- **You don't have to be an extrovert.** Shy people can thrive as housecleaners, although if you're happiest working alone, there are some issues you'll want to consider. Running a housecleaning business will involve time with people. You have to sell your services to new clients, for instance, as well as greet the clients you work with when you arrive in their homes, deal with phone or e-mail inquiries, and so on. And you'll be on your own in these encounters; you won't have a boss or company behind you. Still, the essence of your business is the cleaning itself.

Marketing is probably the hardest part of the job for anyone, shy or not. And you have to do it—you can't clean for clients you don't have! The good news is that it gets easier over time. You get used to it, and you simply have more to talk about: You know what kinds of questions and concerns other clients have had, so you have a pretty good idea of what to say to potential customers. And once you have even a single client, you can focus on providing excellent service. That's the heart of your work; in the end, it's what will get you clients and keep them coming back. It doesn't matter if you're a party animal or utterly tongue-tied. Yes, you have to be prepared for some people time, especially when your business is getting off the ground. If you can handle this, however, your people time will be balanced by plenty of independence and solitude as well.

- **You don't have to be an introvert, either.** If you thrive on contact with people, if conversations leave you energized and happy, you can build your business around these strengths, too. Cleaning does involve a large amount of time spent working on your own, and you will have to deal with that, but you can find ways to build more interaction into your work. Focus on marketing, on networking with other entrepreneurs, on special-events cleaning. Be active in your community. Consider working with a partner or expanding your business by taking on employees. Bottom line: A housecleaning business is what you make it. You'll spend a certain amount of time alone; you'll want to think about this—and your ability to be happy with it—realistically. Then build your business around what you love most.

So what qualities *should* you have to be a top-notch housecleaner? Here are a few that are important:

- **Hardworking.** Owning a business is very hard work, and owning a housecleaning business is even harder. Are you ready to give up free time to do administrative work or to distribute flyers door to door? Will you want to spend evenings or weekends answering phone inquiries, preparing mailings, or giving estimates? Make sure you have a realistic picture of what business ownership will be like before you leap in.
- **Disciplined.** You don't get sick days in this business (at least not paid ones), and you don't get paid vacations or personal time either. If you don't show up, you don't get paid—and you lose clients fast. As a service provider, living up to your commitments is your job description. Do it and you'll succeed. Don't and you won't.
- **Conscientious.** Clients may have different cleaning standards than you do, and you have to meet them. If you walk into a room that looks clean enough to perform surgery in, would you blow off cleaning it, or would you roll up your sleeves and get to work because that's your job? If it's the end of the day and you're beat, would you take a few shortcuts cleaning that kitchen, or would you buckle down and give it the full treatment? Clients may never notice all the things you do clean, but they sure will notice everything you don't.

- **Able to keep a secret.** You will—trust us—learn a lot of confidential information about people on this job. It's critical that you keep this information to yourself. If your clients don't trust you, you don't have a business. That said, there are some secrets that shouldn't be ignored, and you'll want to consider getting outside help to deal with them. Domestic abuse, child abuse, drug abuse, criminal activity—it's unlikely that you'll confront any of these, but it is possible. Be prepared to face some complicated and difficult decisions. (Just don't face them alone. Get the advice of someone you trust. See chapter 4 for more.)
- **Personal boundaries.** This will help you out a lot. As an entrepreneur, you'll be sacrificing a lot of your time and energy—but save some for yourself. It's important to know how to say no. Know what kinds of behavior are acceptable to you and what kinds aren't. Don't expect your clients to be your friends. (For more about boundaries, see chapter 5.)
- **Support system.** Any business can be a lonely, scary venture, not to men-

---

Top Ten Reasons to Be a Housecleaner

1. **Immediate gratification.** Walk in and a house is dirty. Walk out and it's sparkling clean. That's a good feeling. Every single housecleaner we've spoken with has listed "sense of accomplishment" as the best part of the job.
2. **Meeting people's needs.** Not only can you enjoy your own satisfaction at a clean house, but you can also know that your clients are enjoying it!
3. **Meaning.** Those cleaners who are going green—and that's just about everyone these days, to some degree!—take pride in knowing that every toilet scrubbed, every client educated, makes the planet a healthier place.
4. **Setting your own hours.** To a large degree, you can tailor your schedule to meet your needs. Want to be home when the kids get out of school? Arrange for it.

5. **Meeting new people.** You'll meet all sorts of people in this job, from every walk of life, including some you might otherwise never get to know.

6. **Variety.** No two days are ever the same.

7. **Pride.** Here's a chance to be the very best you can be—in a business that you own.

8. **Tax breaks.** You may be able to deduct many of your expenses from your tax bill (see chapter 11).

9. **Minimal start-up cost.** The more seed money you have, the better (naturally!), but you can in fact get started in this business for the cost of transportation to your first client's home.

10. **Profits!** You can make a good living cleaning houses—and some people make a great living.

tion exhausting, frustrating, discouraging, and, yes, sometimes exhilarating, too. The more people you have around to share all these emotions with, the better off you'll be. Having the support of your spouse and children can make or break a business, and there's no substitute for a network of friends who listen, encourage, commiserate, celebrate, and give foot rubs. If you're lacking in the support department—recently divorced or new to an area, for example—see chapter 6 for some ideas about how to help take care of yourself. Consider working with a partner (or three) as well. Everything— transportation, scheduling, heavy lifting, and those all-important complain-and-popcorn sessions—is easier when it's shared.

02 Getting Started I: The Legalities

So you've decided that a home-based housecleaning business is right for you—congratulations!

It's time now to build the foundation for your new business. The weeks or months you put into your home-based business *before* you clean a single house can in fact make or break your future. The process starts with understanding and following the legal requirements for your operations.

Although you might be a micro enterprise, this doesn't mean that you are at any time exempt from adhering to government rules and regulations when it comes to forming, operating, and paying taxes on your home business.

The first tangible step is usually applying for a business name and license. Before you can do this, however, there's another decision for you to make.

What Kind of Business Am I?

There's more than one way to own a business. Before applying for a license, you must be clear on your business's type of ownership. The designation usually depends on the type of service or product being offered. Most small home-based businesses are sole proprietorships.

Other types of businesses are corporations, partnerships, and limited liability companies (LLCs).

In most cases a sole proprietorship is appropriate for a home-based cleaning business. Being a sole proprietor simply means that you are the owner of the business and that you aren't entering into a partnership or corporation. These terms can be confusing if you're not familiar with them, so here are the basics.

Sole Proprietor

A sole proprietorship is a structure that identifies you as legally doing business. In a sole proprietorship, federal and state income tax laws view you and your business as one entity. The business can only be owned by you (although in some states a sole proprietorship can be extended to include a spouse). For a one-person business that does not generate more than a million dollars a year, a sole proprietorship makes the most sense.

A sole proprietorship is also the most inexpensive type of business to start up. Your business taxes are paid through the personal income taxes that you file at year end. Any losses that you have suffered as a sole proprietor can be deducted from your annual income tax. The business and personal taxes are calculated at the same rate. Your business earnings are considered to be your personal earnings, so the more prosperous your business, the higher the rate of personal taxation. That's not a bad thing! Consider that if you worked for a corporation and earned $50,000 a year, you'd be in a higher tax bracket than if you earned $50,000 in profits from a home business. This is because as a business owner, you'll be making plenty of itemized tax deductions, so your overall profit and bottom line will be lower than if you earned the same salary working for someone else. (There's more on taxes in chapter 11.)

The downside is that if you can't pay debts that were incurred as operational expenses for your business, or if your business fails, not only will your business assets be at stake, but your personal assets can also be seized to pay off the debts. Personal assets include property such as real estate, as well as belongings such as a coin collection. If the sole proprietor dies, the business dies with her or him. Many new business owners worry about losses that might be accrued in the wake of a lawsuit. This shouldn't be an issue for you, however; you can purchase liability insurance to cover you in the case of lawsuits, even up to a million dollars. (See chapter 12 for more on insurance.) You can rest assured that your property will not be seized if you ruin someone's kitchen sink.

Corporation

Corporations are very complicated, and forming one is costly. The general difference between a sole proprietorship and a corporation is that a corporation has a lot more money at risk, so it must exist as a legal entity separate from its owner. In doing so, the corporation gains a few advantages, but at a heavy cost. For example, a profitable corporation would be able to issue company stock. The selling and trading of stock is regulated by the Internal Revenue Service as well as at the state level, so simply getting the go-ahead to trade stocks could cost the corporation hundreds of thousands of dollars. In another instance, should a corporation be sued—say, in a class-action lawsuit—the owner would be protected from liens that might otherwise be placed against her or his personal property. It is unlikely that a small home business would ever generate enough profit (we're talking in the million-dollar range) to sell stock or to worry about a class-action lawsuit.

On the other hand, no one person in a corporation can be held liable for business debts or actions. If an owner dies, the corporation is not affected. In the case of a corporate bankruptcy, business assets can be seized, but not personal property or assets. Depending on the scope of the business, a corporation can seek either federal or state incorporation. Incorporating requires a lawyer and the accompanying hefty legal fees.

Our advice? Don't incorporate your business at start-up; the money and headaches far outweigh the benefits. Still, it's an interesting option to keep in mind for the future, especially if your company really takes off.

Partnership

In this ownership structure, you legally partner with at least one other person to conduct the business as co-owners. All parties are seen as equal and responsible entities. They equally share the business losses and liabilities as well as the profits. Each partner pays business income taxes in relation to her or his specific percentage share in the business. Partnerships can be financially advantageous for larger enterprises, because each partner represents a funding source: the more partners, the more start-up funds. Also, each partner brings a set of individual skills and experiences to the company; each one has something different to offer the business. If the business suffers losses because of one partner, all partners will have to deal with the consequences. If a partner dies or drops out of the partnership, or if a new partner joins, then the existing partnership will dissolve and a new one must be formed. A great amount of trust is needed in order for a partnership to succeed. All too often, partnerships have been the cause of irreconcilable differences, ending in the dissolution of the structure; this is particularly true when family members and friends venture into a partnership. Partnerships can be a legal nightmare. We don't recommend that you form a legal partnership for a new business. You're setting yourself up for heaps of trouble when it comes to dissolving the partnership or even for simple day-to-day operations. In a worst-case scenario, your partner could disappear with the entire bank account, leaving you responsible for the business.

Limited Liability Company (LLC)

LLCs are very complicated and rarely found in a home-business environment. The limited liability company partially protects the business owner by limiting the amount of money and property that the company might lose through lawsuits or bankruptcy. Often the liability is limited to the amount of the investment in the company, and the rules are even more complicated when it comes to the investments of other partners and investors. An LLC would not be an option for a housecleaning business, because you aren't investing hundreds of thousands of dollars, and chances are slim that you'd ever be sued for an amount that exceeds your insurance liability. Also, having one or more partners with large investments would be unlikely. An LLC would be more appropriate for, say, a company that provided financial services across the globe.

Choosing and Registering a Name for Your Company

Deciding on a name for your company isn't as easy as it sounds—most of the unique, catchy names are already taken. Your best bet is to choose three or four names that you like and that reflect a positive image, a first choice and two or three others that you can live with. Then if your top choice is already in use by someone else, you'll have one or more to fall back on.

Here's a tip that will save you a lot of time and trouble when it comes to registering your company's name: Use your last name as part of the company name. This probably won't work as well if your last name is common, such as Jones or Smith. If your last name is unusual, however—say, Smitheron—try something like Smitheron Cleaning. A company that uses the owner's name is less likely to be in use, and it will be easier for people to find your company in the phone book or on the Internet if all they can remember is your last name.

Avoid using generic, clichéd names: Super Cleaners, Kleen Cleaners, Elite Cleaning, Quality Cleaners, and so forth. These names are a dime a dozen; they just don't help you or your company stand out from among the scores of other companies with similar names. Choosing a common and overused name could even cause you to lose business to companies with similar names. Clients who can't remember that you are Elite Cleaning Service might phone Executive Elite Cleaning Services—someone else's firm.

The word *maid* is problematic when it comes to a housecleaning business. Maids are full-service employees and provide more than the general

Overly Generic and Predictable Names:

- Progress Cleaners
- Prompt Cleaners
- Clean and Go
- Sparkle Cleaners
- Executive Maid Service

Great Examples of Simple Yet Memorable Names:

- Cornerstone Cleaning (it's simple yet elegant)
- Boiling Kettle Cleaning Service (boiling kettle, clean water—nice analogy)
- Rags and Roses Cleaners (we can smell the roses, can't you?)
- The Cleaning Agents (the X-Files of housecleaning!)
- SOS Cleaning (the call for help, SOS, is whimsical, but not too cute)

housecleaning services. If you do include *maid* in your name—and many people do, if only because it allows for so many catchy puns on the word *made*—you could receive calls from folks looking for cooking, catering services, and child-care or nanny services. You may well prefer to stick to a company title that represents what you are: a housecleaner.

Once you've come up with a couple of possibilities, what's next? You need to be sure that no one else is using the name you've chosen. There are a few ways to do this. The easiest is to go to the county clerk's office and review the local deed registry to determine whether anyone within your city or town is using the name. You can also do a name search at most libraries for a small fee. If you're using your last name as part of the company's name, and the last name isn't too common, there's a good chance that no one else is using it. Once you've cleared the name at the local registry, you can register your name at the county level; there may be an

Domestic Goddess Cleaning

St. Louis, Missouri
www.domesticgoddesscleaningservice.com
(636) 410-5060

Phil and Sandy Adams started Domestic Goddess Cleaning Service in 2005 with no capital at all—just a strong work ethic, an intense desire to succeed, and (let's not forget) one of the best business names *ever*. That name has had a strong appeal for customers ever since, and Phil stresses what an asset it's been—drawing customers like a magnet. It's smart, it's sassy, it makes you smile—who *wouldn't* trust a Domestic Goddess in their home? That's what you want as a cleaner: to make your customers feel happy about your presence in their lives.

With just their own hard work, the Adamses have built their business to the point that they now hire other cleaners—called "Goddesses," of course—to service their accounts. They have as many as four or five Goddesses working for them at a time, depending on availability (it's a high-turnover business) and the season.

Why do this work? "The sense of accomplishment," says Phil. "You come into a nasty house, and when you leave it's clean and fresh. It even smells good." That's a strong motivator—every day. It may be more than a cubicle worker gets in a month or even a year.

The worst part? "Doing the work!" Phil says with a laugh. "This is not an easy job. If you're looking to be a housecleaner, you definitely want to be strong."

The Adamses have had great success with their Web site. "About 95 percent of our customers come to us through the site," Phil notes. According to the Adamses, however, it's best to stick to a site you control yourself. Of those Web services or directories that charge you for each lead generated, "If you pay more than a dollar a lead, it's not worth it," Phil believes.

He's enthusiastic about the prospects for housecleaning as a career, especially in a shaky economy, pointing out the flexibility it offers—"You can start small, and your success depends on how hard you're willing to work." Almost any personality—a people person, a shy person, a leader, a follower—can shine in this industry; the only nonnegotiable requirement is a tireless work ethic. Indeed, there's something appealing about a field that rewards you directly for the commitment you put in. More commitment, more care, more pride equals more success. It's an equation that makes for a very satisfying workday. "The stronger your work ethic, the better the chance your business will grow."

Phil and Sandy offer one last tip: Recommend to clients that they change their furnace filter. Frequently. Regularly. "If more people did that, we'd be out of a job!" Phil says, grinning. Exactly the kind of advice customers will love to get from you.

additional small fee. This means that no one else can come along and legally use your company's name.

The next step is to proceed to the state level. You can have the secretary of state's office take care of a state business name search and registration (for a small fee); in many states you can also conduct a search online. (To find the appropriate Web site, enter "secretary of state" and your state name into any search engine.) Once you receive documentation that the name is not being used, you can file for state registration. (Again, a fee may be charged.) The name is then yours to use.

Most people stop registering at the state level. Because your cleaning business is a local business and not one in which you're shipping products or retailing items worldwide, there really is no reason to patent or trademark the name. However, you do want to be sure that you are not infringing on someone else's trademark. If you want to register "Tompkins' Cleaning Crew" in Utah and both the local and state searches turn up clear, you also want to do a search with the Patent and Trademark Office (PTO) located in Washington, D.C. You can get the forms by mail or on the Web site (www.uspto.gov); most libraries can also provide you with either the paperwork or a full-service search. If the PTO search reveals that the name Tompkins' Cleaning Crew is patented by someone in Massachusetts, you cannot legally use the name. That would be like opening up a hamburger stand and calling it McDonald's Burgers (even if your last name is McDonald).

Patents and trademarks are not common in sole proprietorships. They're expensive to file, the paperwork can be exhausting, and they usually require an attorney's intervention, so most people don't bother. As long as you aren't infringing on some-one's trademark, you needn't worry about getting a patent on your own business name. In the United States there may be 11,000 companies with the name Tomp-kins' Cleaning Crew. Provided none of these companies is doing business in your town or the next county, it's perfectly fine for all of you to coexist without having to worry about patent or trademark infringement—if, that is, no one has applied for and received a patented trademark for the business use of the name.

The next step is to file for a fictitious business name. This sounds a bit frighten-ing, but it takes less than fifteen minutes and costs less than $100. It is required if you're doing business using any name other than your own. Some people deliber-ately keep their entire name as the name of the business in order to avoid having to file for a fictitious business name. For example, a sole proprietorship named Joe Normandy would not have to file as a fictitious business because Joe Normandy is not fictitious. Joe Normandy's Cleaning Company, however, would have to file a fic-titious business name registration because, of course, there's no person named Joe Normandy's Cleaning Company.

The problem with simply using your full name, however, is this: Who would make the connection between Joe Normandy and a cleaning business? Using a full name might work for a restaurant or an artist, but not in the cleaning industry. Without mentioning cleaning or cleaners in conjunction with your last name, clients will have no idea what sort of service you provide.

Filing for a fictitious business name serves several purposes. For one, it estab-lishes you as a community business. Once you file, you are required to place an ad in a local newspaper to announce your DBA (doing business as). This is a practice dat-ing back to colonial times. In the colonial era, tradesmen (women were not allowed to own businesses) and artisans often had similar names and trades that made it impossible to discern who owned which business. For example, there could have been forty-two blacksmiths named John Brown who lived in colonial Boston. Placing a newspaper statement would clarify which John Brown, residing at which address, owned the blacksmith shop on 12th Street. The newspaper ad as well as the actual on-file fictitious business name document make it easy for people to find you, the owner of the company.

In general, the only people who need to find you would be customers who wish to lodge a complaint against an unknown company owner, or those wishing to obtain your mailing address so that they can bombard you with investment opportunities and sales pitches. A fictitious business name document is freely available to the public. Consider also that a person wishing to open a business using the same name as yours—say, Sunshine Cleaning Service—will have the right to do so if you haven't registered the name.

The second purpose of the fictitious business name document is that it's required in order to open a business bank account, as well as to maintain business accounts for credit or invoicing. Without the document, most banks will refuse to open an account, while some may open the account but place a hold on it until they have received a copy of the document. Or worst of all, the bank will open a business account for you without the document, and you'll have no trouble for years, until you receive a letter from the bank stating that your account is frozen because it was discovered that your file is missing a copy of your fictitious name registration document. It will take you weeks to file and receive the document in order to regain control of your bank account. And that's assuming that in the years since you started your business, no one else has come along and filed a fictitious name document that uses the same name as your business!

Remember also that many stores and online retailers in the cleaning industry will open a business credit account for you, enabling you to purchase supplies at a generous discount. To prevent misrepresentation, the companies will require your fictitious name registration number. You can't afford not to have the document when it comes to discounted supplies.

The third and most important function of the document is that you have no legal standing without it. For example, let's say that you are John Jones, the owner of Sunshine Cleaning Services. Two months ago a client responded to a Sunshine Cleaning Service business card that you posted in the supermarket. You rendered service to the client and left a bill. You did not receive a check in the mail, so you billed the client again, and again. The client ignored subsequent bills and telephone calls. You decide to take the client to small claims court to recoup your fee, plus late charges. You fill out the appropriate papers at the courthouse and pay the filing fee. The clerk asks for your fictitious name registration form or number. You don't have one. You're out of luck. In the court's eyes, Sunshine Cleaners performed the service, and Sunshine Cleaners, not John Jones, is the payee for the service. Therefore, Sunshine Cleaners is the only entity that can file a claim and bring the nonpaying client to court, and in the court's view, Sunshine Cleaners doesn't exist. You don't want to be met with a situation like this.

1. The name as you wish it to be registered: _____

_____

2. A brief statement of the character or nature of the business or other activity to be carried on under or through the fictitious name: _____

_____

_____

_____

_____

3. The mailing address of the business (this address does not have to be the principal place of business and can be directed to anyone's attention): _____

_____

_____

_____

4. The county where the principal place of business of the fictitious name is located. If there is more than one county, list all applicable counties or state "multiple": _____

_____

_____

_____

5. Federal Employer Identification (FEI) number if known or if applicable: _____

_____

6. Owner's name, address, and Social Security number (the Social Security number is not mandatory): _____

_____

_____

_____

Owner's signature _____

Daytime telephone number _____

Applying for a Business License

With your ownership decided and your name registered, you're ready to receive a business license. The legal criteria for these licenses vary from state to state, county to county, city to city. Check with your local county clerk for information specific to your locality. As the owner of a business, you must comply with all federal, state, and local regulations. You must also register your business in order to file tax documents. Without the proper license and registration, you are not a legitimate business and therefore not entitled to any of the federal or state tax opportunities.

Unfortunately, obtaining a license is where many housecleaning businesses fall short. This is where professionals are separated from the work-for-cash sorts of operations. If anything were to happen—such as a lawsuit—and it were discovered that you were operating an unlicensed business, you'd be setting yourself up for some pretty hefty fines as well as embarrassment. Sole proprietorships are relatively easy to register and license. Difficulties occur only when the sole proprietor is retailing a product such as food or clothing or when a regulated service such as child care or hairstyling is involved. Housecleaning services are not regulated, and you are not retailing regulated products or services, so the process is fairly simple.

Remember, a business license only allows you to legally operate a business within a specified locale; it does not license you as housecleaner. Sometimes clients will see the term *licensed* on your business card and misinterpret it as meaning that you're certified by an accrediting source to perform the duties of a housecleaner. Some vocational trades do require job-specific certification at the state level. For example, in addition to registering and licensing as a business, hairstylists and electricians must pass a written exam to obtain a license to ply their trade. There are no accrediting sources for housecleaners—although you will find some cleaning personnel who work within major chemical industry facilities, such as a chemical treatment plant or hazardous waste facility, who've received college degrees and certifications in sanitation and waste management. Let's hope that you can stick to cleaning soap scum and window grime: Hazardous waste cleaning is dangerous! Some states' license applications are ten pages long, while those from other states are only half a page. The two most important questions on the application are about what type of business you're licensing and where you intend to do business. In most cities and states, you can register a sole proprietorship for less than $250 a year.

Business License FAQ

Do I need a business license even if my business is home-based and I have no employees?

Yes. All persons conducting a business must register a sole proprietor business license application.

Do I need a license even if I'm doing business simply under my own name?

If you're simply cleaning under your own name, you usually don't need a license, but this varies from locale to locale, so you'll want to check. Still, you're much better off doing business under a business name. Take the time to register your business; it's worth it.

Do I need a license from my state, county, and city?

Procedures vary around the country; you'll have to do the research about your own location. Start with your town or county clerk or with a librarian. The Small Business Administration is also a good place to turn to for information and help on licensing; see "Appendix II: Resources" in the back of this book.

Where am I permitted to do business?

Some states have zoning policies that will not allow you to do business outside of the jurisdiction of certain counties and townships without applying for separate licenses. Most states do not. For those states that require multiple licensure for adjacent areas, the fees are generally low: between $15 and $100.

Setting Up a Business Bank Account

In the past banks made it very difficult for small businesses to maintain a checking or savings account. Only a few years ago, it was common for small-business owners to ask clients to make checks payable to the owner rather than to the business. Who could have blamed them, when banks were charging inflated fees simply to deposit a single check?

Happily, those days are gone. Today most small-business accounts come with a variety of options for fees and account maintenance. Still, business accounts are nowhere near as flexible as personal accounts. You'll want to research several banks to find one that meets your needs, with low costs and no hidden fees.

Name: _____

E-mail address: _____

_____

Business Information

Name of business: _____

Mailing address: _____

_____

_____

Property address: _____

_____

_____

Telephone numbers: _____

_____

_____

Federal employer tax ID number: _____

State sales tax ID number: _____

Type of ownership: _____

State registration/license number: _____

Number of employees: _____

Type of business (please describe in detail products and services provided): ___

_____

_____

_____

_____

_____

If a professional license is required, list the license type, license number, name of license holder, and his or her position in the business: _____

_____

_____

_____

_____

_____

Does this business export a product or service to a foreign country? _____

_____

Does this business sell tobacco products as a retailer? _____

_____

Owner Information

Owner 1 name: _____

_____

Address: _____

_____

_____

Owner 2 name: _____

_____

Address: _____

_____

_____

Emergency Contacts

Names and telephone numbers of people (managers, key holders) to contact in case of an emergency (such as fire or robbery)

Name:

_____

Telephone:

_____

Name:

_____

Telephone:

_____

While you're comparison shopping, it's a good idea to find out whether a bank can offer you a merchant credit card account in addition to your business account. A merchant account would allow clients to pay with a credit card. If you're planning to offer this payment option to clients—now or in the future—it can be a real convenience to do so through a single bank. There's more about merchant accounts later in this chapter.

Bank Shopping

When comparing banks' business account rates, a new proprietor of a service-oriented business is likely to think, *I don't need a checking account, because I'm not going to write checks from the account.* Although it's true that you might never write a single check from a business checking account, it's still the best way to go. It's inexpensive to maintain, and you don't need to order boxes of checks—you won't need them.

One of the best ways to keep fees to a minimum is to query the bank where you currently hold your personal accounts. If you're already a customer in good standing, most banks will allow you to open a business checking account and link it to your personal checking or savings account. This way, you need only make deposits into your business account and then transfer funds once or twice a month from the business account into your personal account. Many banks now offer the option of transferring funds and accessing your accounts online. Remember to keep personal and business-related banking separate. Use your business account only for your business.

Business Account Paperwork

Most of the low-fee business accounts out there are simplified checking accounts. A simplified business checking account is generally used for a sole proprietorship that deposits fewer than a hundred items per month, and has no complicated business dealings such as tax liens, letters of credit requesting high escrow, or questionable international transactions. You should know that over the past decade or so, simple business checking accounts have been used by illegal money laundering operations, so don't be offended if a bank representative asks you, "What is the nature of your business?" The representative is required by federal law to ask, as well as to keep a written record of your answer.

When you open the account, you're opening it as a sole proprietorship with a DBA (doing business as)—your fictitious business name statement. Not all banks require the documentation, but it's a good idea to get the DBA before making a trip to the bank. By doing so, you won't be in for any surprises, and you'll appear as an organized, professional business owner. In most states, a sole proprietor uses her or his Social Security number to serve as the employer identification number (EIN). When you file income tax, you and your business are one and the same. Thus you can deduct your business losses against your total household income.

Most simple business checking accounts require a small minimum balance—usually between $100 and $250—and are usually non-interest-bearing. So you'll want to develop a schedule to transfer the funds from the non-interest-bearing business account into an interest-bearing account, such as your personal savings account. The sooner you can transfer the funds to an interest-bearing account, the more money you'll be able to save.

Be careful not to exceed your monthly transaction limit. Transaction limits range from seventy-five to one hundred, and the transfer of funds to another account is indeed counted as a transaction. Here are a couple of examples of typical business account structures. What you find at your bank may, of course, be different.

Account Example 1

Monthly fee (waived with minimum balance) $12

Minimum average daily balance to waive monthly fee $7,500

Line of credit overdraft protection?   No

Savings overdraft protection?   Yes

Fee per transaction $1.00 after the first 75 transactions per month

Account Example 2

Monthly fee (waived with minimum balance) $25

Minimum average daily balance to waive monthly fee $100

Line of credit overdraft protection?   No

Savings overdraft protection?   Yes

Fee per transaction $0.25 after the first 100 transactions per month

Receiving Payments by Credit Card

Many financial institutions offer something called merchant accounts, which allow you to accept payment by credit card. The application process is fairly simple and straightforward. You'll want to shop around, however, because different banks offer different terms. Ask about each bank's fees, including per-item fees, supply fees, and statement fees. Make sure you understand the process thoroughly, and know who to contact in case of problems or questions.

The scariest part of a business is getting started.

How do you find the clients? How do you provide referrals if you're just starting out? How do you set fees that are comparable to those of your competitors? It's enough to send you running for the Pepto-Bismol! Still, taking it one step at a time, along with being highly organized, will get you moving in the right direction in no time.

Setting Fees

Fee setting is tricky—for housecleaning and for any service. If you ever need a room in your home painted, for instance, you can call dozens of painters, each of whom will give you a different price. You might receive estimates ranging from $300 to $2,000 for the same labor and supplies. Some painters will price their assignments by the hour, others by the job. One hourly painter might charge $30 while another charges $200.

Housecleaning businesses are similar: Some charge by the assignment and some by the hour. Some even charge by the quarter hour. You'll find that one cleaner charges $50 for a four-hour job, while another charges $150.

Why such extreme fluctuations? One reason is that many housecleaning businesses operate with several employees. With each employee comes increased expenses for liability insurance, bonding, transportation reimbursement, cell phones, and so forth. In order for the proprietor to turn a profit, the client charges have to more than adequately cover expenses. Expanding your business by adding employees thus isn't always a wise business choice. While a multistaffed cleaning business might charge $150 to clean a six-room home, a sole proprietor could charge $75 for the same job. If your services are priced out of range, clients will balk at hiring you. A wise consumer would look for services that fall somewhere in the middle price range. Goods or services that cost more aren't necessarily better.

The first step in fee setting is to have a realistic estimate of your actual expenses, including insurance, licensure, supplies, equipment, advertising, and so on. If your fees don't cover your expenses, you're obviously going to have problems, and fast! Keep a monthly expense record to estimate your own expenses for three months. Be as accurate and realistic as you can; wherever possible, do the research and plug in the actual expense amounts (for licenses, insurance and bonding policies, and the like), not just estimates. Once you have an idea of how much money you'll be spending to stay in business, you'll have a beginning point from which to calculate your fees.

Many other factors go into fee setting besides expenses, including the needs of your specific locale. The prices of goods and services in cities and areas with large populations are higher than in areas with smaller populations where there's less demand for the same goods and services. If you live in a rural area, take transportation into consideration. Will you need to drive long distances to get to clients' homes? Do the clients live on the opposite ends of town? If you're servicing two clients on the same day, does it take you forty minutes or longer to get from the home of client A to the home of client B? If you'll be spending three hours a day driving, then your fees must adequately compensate you for those hours.

How much competition do you have? Are you finding that you have to drive to the next county in order to secure clients at all? Or are people snapping up your service like hotcakes? Are you utterly exhausted at the end of the day, with little profit to show for it? It takes time and experience in order to know exactly what sort of fees will bring the best results. Rest assured that you will gain the experience, and in no time you'll feel like an old pro!

Here's one last piece of advice: Don't be afraid to charge the fees you deserve. Yes, you might want to start on the lower end if you're new to the business, then raise your fees as you gain experience. But don't undersell yourself. You will work very hard as a housecleaner, and what you do is important to your clients. You are worth the money you charge!

Learning from the Competition

Get to know your competitors: who they are, what they do, and what they charge. Gather information from all possible advertising venues: Web sites, newspapers,

Yellow Pages, business cards from bulletin boards, flyers that have been posted at the supermarket, and so on. You should be able to come up with a list of all the housecleaning service providers in your immediate area. On a card, record the name, telephone number, and Internet address of fifteen or so of the businesses, as well as the name and title of the contact person. Visit the companies' Web sites, and then spend an afternoon calling these businesses. Posing as a potential customer, get as much information as you can without raising suspicion. The businesses are open to the public, and anyone has the right to make a simple inquiry. Ask the following questions and record the answers on your index cards:

- *How soon could I obtain an estimate for housecleaning?* Is the next appointment for an estimate six months away or next Friday?
- *Do you charge by the hour or by the job? If hourly, what is the rate?* Service providers who charge by the hour get their hourly wage whether the job was completed or not.
- *Is there a minimum number of hours required?* Most housecleaners will require at least two hours.
- *How are routine visits scheduled?* Perhaps the company serves the north end of the city on Monday and Tuesday, or perhaps apartments are done on Thursday and Friday, while large homes are done only on Wednesday and Thursday.
- *Do you serve my area? If not, what is the zone of service?* Will the company accommodate potential out-of-zone clients for an added fee?
- *Are you insured and bonded?* Ask for the name of the provider and an account number so that you can phone to confirm the information.
- *How long have you been in business?*
- *Do you offer written information about your services, procedures, and policies?*
- *What are the payment options?*
- *Do you have employees or does the owner complete the assignments?* If there are employees, are they insured and bonded as well? How long have the employees been with the company?

If the person says that she or he will call you back or will e-mail you with answers and doesn't, be sure to note that on your card, too. Get a sense of how you were treated. Did the person seem bored or irritated that you called or wrote? If the person spoke to you in a gruff or frustrated tone, then perhaps business isn't going well—or maybe it's going too well. A negative impression could indicate problems with the service, and you need to record this on the index card. There may come a time when you're overloaded with business and need to network with other housecleaners to exchange client referrals. You certainly don't want to refer an inappropriate service provider to a potential client!

Don't discount someone who won't disclose information on the telephone, preferring instead to do an in-home consultation prior to discussing rates and availability. Insisting on an in-home consultation or estimate is the sign of an organized and professional housecleaner. Although you won't be able to get the information without a consultation, you'll at least have an idea of the sorts of professionals you will be competing with.

Be aware, too, that proprietors may be justifiably nervous about disclosing information if they sense you're a competitor. You really can't ask someone to spill the tricks of the trade so that you can then offer the same services for a reduced price. That's called undercutting, and it's unethical. So be professional, and gather whatever information you can by telephone or online. You'll get a pretty good idea of what others are doing and how they are doing it. But do use the information responsibly.

Getting the First Client or Two

When you go out for your first consultation, the potential client will inevitably want to know the extent of your experience, how long you've been in business, and how many clients you currently serve. Few people want to be the first client. So how do you round up enough experience so that the first potential client doesn't feel like an experiment? We have a couple of great suggestions.

Volunteer to Clean the Home of a Friend or Family Member

Friends and family members are your best resources! Perhaps someone in your circle of friends or relatives has recently had a baby, has taken a new job with long hours, or is overwhelmed with night classes and a heavy daytime schedule. Offer to give the person a break by doing some free housecleaning. Explain that you're building up clientele, and that you could benefit from both the experience and the feedback. Most people understand that starting a business isn't easy, and that everyone needs to start somewhere. If you feel uncomfortable making the offer, choose people who are close to you and who don't mind that you'll be in their personal space for a few hours.

When you perform the service for a friend or relative, treat the job as if it were for a paying client. Ask for feedback on the assignment. Did the service provided meet the assumed client's needs and expectations? Was the service flawless? Consider practice cleaning not only as helpful lessons in learning to accept constructive criticism and feedback but also as practice in learning to establish ETTs (estimated time on tasks). In which rooms did you feel you may have spent too much time, and in which areas could you have spent more time? Be sure to ask these "clients" for permission to use them as references!

Volunteer to Clean for a Nonprofit Organization

This is another wonderful way to gain experience and references, and it will benefit the community at the same time. Check with any organizations that you already belong to and see if they'll let you volunteer a few hours of your time to clean an office, dining hall, lobby, or conference room. Here are some organizations you might want to contact about donating cleaning services:

- a church, temple, or other place of worship
- the Salvation Army or any local shelter or social-service-based program
- schools
- social groups and lodges (for example, the Masonic Temple or the Girl Scouts)
- libraries
- thrift stores

You can also do some research to find community groups that are planning fund-raising events such as flea markets or silent auctions for charity. People donate items such as furniture, books, and toys to be sold at such events, and many local businesses donate services, which go to the highest bidder. Consider donating a coupon for a free housecleaning. The winning bidder could become a longtime client and might eventually refer you to others.

Getting started isn't as complicated as you might think. It is time consuming, and the research can be frustrating, but you already know that if you want to launch your business with as few problems as possible, you'll have to work at it. Remember that you are building a business, and you'll be working harder for yourself than you ever did for anyone else. So take no shortcuts, and you'll have few surprises.

How to Get a Business Logo

Early on in the life of your business, although not necessarily before start-up, you'll want a logo. A business logo identifies your company. Think of a few well-known and popular company logos—the Morton's salt girl, AOL's blue triangle, the Nike swoosh—and of how consumers have come to acquaint such logos with a history of quality products and services.

Your logo will also come to reflect your business's positive history. Designing a logo can be tough, though, especially if you aren't artistically inclined. If you can draw a pretty good stick figure but are otherwise hopeless, you'll need outside help. If you were to hire a graphic arts company to design your logo, you would be looking at a bill of several hundred to several thousand dollars. You must pay for the graphic designer's time—either hourly or as a flat fee per assignment—as well as for the production service: ink, computer software, plates, and so forth. A designer will usually draft three samples. If you don't like any of the three, then you'll pay an extra charge for the next set of samples. Remember that the fees do not include printing services. The designer will deliver a completed logo on a CD-ROM; it's your responsibility to find an affordable printer for business cards, brochures, and letterhead.

But there are other sources. One simple solution is to check with your friends and family members. Going with someone you know is often your best bet, because the person already has an idea of the sorts of things you like. Even if the artist is a friend or family member, don't expect the service or final product to be free. Artists are professionals just like you, and are entitled to receive payment for services rendered. Offer to pay for the service, or suggest that you barter your service for theirs. (Please note, by the way, that the IRS treats barter income just like regular income: You must declare the value of the product or service you receive on your taxes.)

If you can't identify any sources, you can extend your search into the online freelance community. Freelancers—also known as consultants, outsourcers, and free agents—are artists who offer their services on a per-assignment basis. There are several online sources of freelance artists. Here are a few that have been around for quite a while and have positive feedback within the online community:

- www.elance.com
- www.buyerzone.com
- www.allcreativeportfolios.com

Each online community works slightly differently, but here's a rough summary of what you can expect:

- You post a job description that details what you want, when you need the work to be completed, and how much you're willing to pay. You might be charged a small fee to post the ad.
- If an artist is interested in your job, she or he will e-mail you for more information and also provide samples of work for you (either at a Web site or as e-mail attachments). Some of the online communities include online portfolios as part of each artist's profile.
- If you like the work of a particular artist and find that you can work with her or him, you enter into a contract. Either you or the artist can draw up a simple one-page contract that can be e-mailed, signed, and copies scanned or faxed. The contract is between you and the artist, not the sponsor of the freelance database.
- In most cases you'll pay a deposit fee. Most of the owners of online databases offer an escrow service: They will hold on to all funds and disburse them upon completion. If the artist is new to the community, or if you're nervous about paying someone who might disappear before your project is delivered, by all means use the escrow service. The cost is minimal and usually a flat fee. This also protects the artist in case you back out of the contract.

- Pay by credit card whenever possible. Doing so gives you recourse if you experience problems with the artist. Most freelancers are linked with one of the many online credit-card-processing companies, so it's easy to send and receive credit card orders.
- The artist will send you renditions of the logo in stages. You must approve each change and rendition in writing. When the end product is completed and you approve it, you forward the fee minus the deposit, then the project is forwarded to you. It's your responsibility to pay for shipping, handling, and insurance of the logo.

If you're fortunate enough to live in a city with an art school or art institute, consider posting an ad on the school's bulletin board. Give the school a call to find out which department approves such postings; usually it's the office of the registrar or job referral center. You can put all of your information onto a 5-by-7-inch index card, or submit a flyer for posting approval. The school will keep a copy of the posting on file. This protects you and the school if someone were to alter the advertisement—say, changing your dollar figure of $150 to $1,500.

Using a student as the designer of your logo can be beneficial to both of you. You'll be able to get a quality piece of art at a reasonable price, and the student will benefit from the income as well as being able to build her or his portfolio of designs.

Melinda's Story

When I first started my business, there was no way that I could afford to pay more than a few hundred dollars for a professional logo, yet I managed to get my logo for free. One of my clients was a graphic artist for a computer firm. I asked him if he could suggest an affordable designer. He offered his own services for a very reduced fee, then I asked if he'd care to barter his designing services for my housecleaning. He couldn't say yes fast enough. He charged me about $200, and I gave him credit for four housecleaning visits. Simply put, he would have paid me for my service, and I'd have paid him for his, so there was no loss whatsoever. I received a beautiful logo customized just for me. I still use it today.

Student designers may ask to use your logo as a class project that will be submitted for a grade. If the student asks for your written permission, by all means agree to it.

When it comes to the logo itself, keep the design as simple as possible. The least expensive design is black on white, either a pen-and-ink design or a computer-generated model. Black on white easily reproduces in newspapers, online, and on

The Victorian Housecleaner

If you think cleaning today is rough, imagine what life as a housecleaner was like during the Victorian era. There were no vacuum cleaners or washing machines, and there was no such thing as central heat or indoor plumbing. You had to warm your home with coal-burning stoves, which filled the air with smoke, smut, and ash. The soot from the coal soiled the furniture, draperies, floor, walls, and ceilings. If the soot wasn't cleaned daily, it permanently stained surfaces; even worse, if allowed to linger, it became a dangerous respiratory irritant. The removal of soot and ash was backbreaking work. Only affluent families could afford a housemaid to come into the home to keep on top of the cleaning chores. In fact, a family's social status was determined by the ability to employ servants. Multiple servants were a sign of wealth. Domestic service was a widespread vocational choice; actually, it was the only employment legal for women.

business cards and brochures. Logos with color are visually appealing and make wonderful choices, but keep in mind that when you use color it will cost you more in professional printing fees. Even if you choose to print business cards, brochures, and letterhead from your own computer, the color ink cartridge will need to be replaced frequently, and this is expensive.

If money is tight as you start up your business, don't worry about waiting a few months before pursuing a logo. You want the most professional piece of art you can get, so wait until you can afford to spring for it. Don't cut corners and resort to using the copyright-free clip art available on the Web and in stores. Anyone can use clip art—the images are a dime a dozen. Don't sell yourself short when it comes to creating a unique image for your business!

Portland, Oregon
(503) 729-9943
www.experiencegreentoday.com

Experience Green

Experience Green opened its doors in Portland, Oregon, in July 2008, and by all accounts has been a meteoric success. It's so busy, in fact, that owners David and Mary not only just hired their first employee, but they also have plans to hire one or two more *each month,* for the next six months.

The company serves both residential and commercial clients in the Portland metro area. David and Mary also offer their own line of green cleaning products—natural cleaners that smell wonderful, are healthy for the planet, and just plain work.

The idea of founding a green cleaning company percolated in the backs of their minds for years. About twelve months before the official launch, David and Mary began pursuing their business plans in earnest and putting the blueprint on paper. "We researched," says Mary. "We researched like crazy." Together the couple pursued both sides of their business equation: Creating a sound, solid, detailed plan for the firm on the one hand, and developing real expertise in environmentally sound cleaning methods and products on the other.

"Get your ducks in a row before you get started," Mary stresses. "Create a solid foundation, just as you would in a house." David chimes in: "That foundation is extremely important. Your business plan should be the center of it. Know exactly where you want to go and how you want to get there."

Back to Mary: "All of our administrative work was put into place before we cleaned a single house. Licensing, EIN [employee identification number], state registration, invoicing, creating invoices, flyers, and job detail forms—not to mention the detailed business plan—we had all of that down in writing." The couple also began reaching out to potential clients in every venue they could find. "Farmers' markets have been very helpful for us," Mary says. "We went to trade shows, we did networking."

Why? "Because once you start getting busy with the cleaning itself," she replies, "you don't have time for any of that. Put it into place *first.*"

At the same time, they began certification classes with the Green Clean Institute (see chapter 7), whose mission is providing both education and certification in environmentally sound practices. They consider this experience invaluable. "No matter how much you think you know," Mary says, "you have something to learn." She emphasizes the importance of green expertise and commitment. "Know a lot about why there's a need for green cleaning, and about how to clean in ways that benefit the planet." Clients will indeed be looking to you for knowledge; the more you have in place, the higher the level of service you'll be able to provide.

Their location in Oregon has been a big help. "Portland is one of the biggest players in the field when it comes to environmental change," Mary says. "But it's definitely not the only one. Everywhere, people are making changes."

"Starting up the business," David adds, "was pretty nerve-racking, actually. The fear of the unknown can be paralyzing. Having a focus—green—allowed us to concentrate on the purpose behind our company, the greater good we want to accomplish." He concludes, "If you honestly believe what you're doing is going to help others, that focus will drive everything else you do."

They started with minimal capital—"Just enough to buy tools and pay for transportation," according to David. "Keeping our costs low was a big factor. We did it all ourselves; we didn't outsource anything. The business plan, the marketing, all of that. And we fed whatever we made back into the business for the first few months, for sure."

The Web site has been a huge source of customers. "At the very beginning," Mary notes, "we used free online sites such as Craigslist, and those worked well." During their intensive start-up phase, the couple also created their own Web site with the help of GoDaddy.com. Says Mary: "It's our number-one marketing tool."

Also crucial has been their dedication to their clients. "You have to take a lot of pride in what you do," Mary says. "You have to be detail-oriented. This job is all about customer service. Customers complain about previous cleaners not doing good work. They started out strong then began to get lazy. You need real pride in your work to get past that."

Clearly the whole Experience Green team has exactly such pride. And for good reason. David and Mary are convinced that each day they go to work, they make the future a little cleaner, a little healthier, a little better. Who *wouldn't* love a career like that? And who *wouldn't* hire a cleaning company with that kind of passionate, contagious commitment?

04

How to Plan and Develop a Service Manual

Of all business documents, the service manual is the most important. A fully developed service manual explains your service in black and white. A professionally planned and constructed manual will:

- separate you from unprofessional and fly-by-night providers;
- fully explain the services that you provide, as well as those you don't;
- answer frequently asked questions and detail rates, charges, and billing policies; and
- list all contact information for your business.

Most initial contacts will come as a response to your Web site or a newspaper advertisement. Thus your Web page or ad should say, "Call or e-mail for a Guide to Services." *Guide to services, service manual, service contract*—choose whichever title works for you, but in any case the document will serve as a selling tool and a general handbook for your business. Remember to review your service manual often—every three to six months is wise. Certainly your rates will change over time, and you may want to add or revise policies as you learn more about what works best for you. If the manual is kept as a file on your computer, it should be a fairly simple matter to update it and print out fresh copies. What you don't want to do is present your manual to potential clients, then immediately have to point out all the spots where it's outdated or inaccurate. Let your manual evolve with your business.

The following pages describe each section of a typical service manual. You can, of course, make any necessary changes to suit your individual needs and policies. A sample manual is included at the end of this chapter.

Presentation

Present the manual in an attractive three-ring binder. If you have used color in your company logo, try to find color-coordinated binders. You can also use colored paper that complements the colors of your logo and binder. A visually pleasing presentation will set you apart from other cleaners who give clients poorly typed, handwritten, or photocopied service policies, as well as from those who present nothing at all.

Cover Page

The cover page is the first visual representation of your business that a client sees. It shouldn't be cluttered with information, slogans, or artwork. Keep it simple. Put your logo on the cover page, along with the business name, spelled out in a large, bold font. The information should catch the eye at first glance. Don't forget to include the obvious text: GUIDE TO SERVICES or SERVICE MANUAL. You want to be sure that people know what it is they're reading. Below the title, include:

- the full business name;
- the telephone number with area code;
- your Web address;
- an e-mail address;
- the business's mailing address; and
- a one-line statement of appeal.

The statement of appeal should be a simple phrase: *Serving Chicago since 2001,* for instance, or *Serving the community of Bridgeport.* Simply said, the statement adds a friendly air to the cover. It should never be gimmicky or contain a sales pitch.

Mission Statement

Every business needs a mission statement. Whether you're selling cars, practicing law, or cleaning homes, the general public deserves to have some idea of why you're in business.

Mission statements can be difficult to develop. On the one hand, it's tempting to include the standard buzzwords and phrases, but on the other, such statements are overdone, lack personality, and say nothing about your business. Take a look at the mission statements of businesses in your area, whether they're one-person operations or multimillion-dollar corporations. Review a dozen or so to see which ones seem professional to you and which are hokey. Avoid the standard clichés; clients have seen them all before. Put yourself in the client's place. If you were seeking a housecleaner, would you trust someone whose mission statement included unimaginative phrases such as *reliable service* or *honest and friendly*? I hope not. Use positive but unique phrasing. Tell potential clients something they didn't already know about your company!

Samples of Terrific Mission Statements

- Manor Cleaning Service understands that the demands of modern careers and lifestyles can sometimes create a gap in housecleaning. We aim to bridge that gap by providing professional housecleaning services.
- The mission of Hourglass Cleaners is to provide long- and short-term housecleaning services within the Bay Area. We're proud of our community commitment to providing affordable and customized housecleaning services.
- Naturally Clean uses only environmentally safe, healthy products and methods to clean your home. Our goal is to create a clean planet, one clean room at a time.

Helpful Phrasing

Desirable	Run-of-the-Mill
Commitment	We aim to please
Professional	Experienced
Pleased	Satisfied
Prompt	Reliable
Quality	Great/Top-notch
Goal	Want
Affordable	Cheap

Some Not-So-Good Mission Statements

- At Starbright Cleaners our number-one priority is making customers happy! If you want a sparkling-clean home, give us a call. We guarantee our services 100 percent.

This lacks personality. How are you going to make clients happy? What happens if you can't make them happy? By guaranteeing services, you'll be cleaning a lot of houses for free.

> ■ You've tried the rest, now try the best! Unlike other cleaning services, we here at Zip-E Clean do it right the first time. You can't beat our prices! Cleaning houses is what we do best!

This statement inspires negative competition, a sign of a nonprofessional. "You can't beat our prices" isn't much of a sales pitch. People should be inspired to call upon you because you're committed to doing what you do, not because you're willing to do it cheaper than the competition.

The Consultation

In most cases you'll be giving a copy of your service manual to prospective clients prior to meeting or speaking with them in depth. You'll want to let them know what to expect from the consultation. In this section of your service manual, you'll briefly explain what happens at the meeting, how long it usually takes, and what days and times you conduct consultations, as well as any information that the client should have ready.

Clientele

Clients like to see what sort of people you currently provide services for. In this section of the manual, you can list what areas you serve; you might also include an analysis of your customer base (even if that's only one client). Perhaps households with two or more children make up 100 percent of your clientele (if you did only one sample cleaning for someone with two or more children, you're entitled to use that figure). Or maybe 50 percent of your clients are one-person households or people away from the house more than forty hours per week.

Services

This is the heftiest portion of the manual; it might run upward of twenty pages, or you can reduce it to about five. It all depends on how specific you want to be.

We recommend that you be as specific as possible. Somewhere down the line, questions will arise on any issue you haven't considered in your manual. You can start with a few paragraphs that describe the sort of services you offer, and perhaps one paragraph or a short list of services that you do not provide. Be sure to include:

- whether or not you'll work with pets or children roaming the home;
- how you intend to handle cancellations (the client's or yours);
- inclement weather and variances in appointment times due to traffic;
- state and federal laws regarding the handling of chemicals; and
- who is to provide the tools and cleaning products.

Confidentiality and Security

Because you'll be storing clients' house keys, you must tell them how and where you do so. Many new clients will be uncomfortable, at least initially, about someone having a set of keys to their home. Put their minds at ease by describing the sort of safe you use (see chapter 9 for information on safes) and your method of handling keys. You'll also need to assure clients that you hold their e-mail and residential addresses, telephone numbers, and profiles in complete confidentiality. Once you list your business with a newspaper or on a Web site, you'll likely be contacted by all sorts of companies that want to trade customer information with you. Never share this information with anyone. The last thing clients want is to be bombarded with e-mails and telephone solicitors.

Client Mailing List

Here clients are alerted to your biweekly or monthly newsletter (via e-mail or snail mail). Point out the importance of the newsletters, which will inform clients of:

- dates that you may be out of town or on vacation;
- holiday reminders;
- discounts and specials;
- contests;
- anticipated delays: bridge construction, closed roads, and so on; and
- charity and community involvement.

Safety

This is a brief section in which you state how (or if) you'll handle various safety issues.

- Note how you'll handle strangers asking who you are. Sometimes burglars watch a home looking to identify the specific routines of people coming and going.
- Mention whether you'll work among other service providers (child-care provider, roofer, plumber, and the like). Many cleaners opt not to work alongside other providers. Other service people tend to clutter up cleaned rooms, and they can be distracting. Consider also the safety risks: You don't want the babysitter to slip on the kitchen floor that you just mopped, for instance. It's fair to decline to work in a home where other people or service providers are present.
- Clients should be told that they need to give you notice if someone else will be in the home, either working or visiting. You don't want to walk into a home and scare someone (or yourself) because no one was expecting you.
- Clients need to tell you about any safety faults in the home. One client neglected to explain that the kitchen's hot- and cold-water faucets were installed incorrectly: The hot water was located on the right rather than the left. You'll need to know of any plumbing problems, broken steps, exposed wiring, and so forth. When it comes to safety, you can't be too cautious.

Rates

This comes toward the end of the manual. You want people to learn about you and your services before they get to your rates. This is also why the manual does not have a table of contents: Readers will go straight for rates and ignore everything else. Note in this section whether you charge by the hour or by the assignment. Also, don't forget to mention:

- how long the rates are good for (one year, or subject to change without notice);
- weekend and holiday rates; if you don't work on New Year's Day, or if you will work but charge time and a half, let clients know; and
- discounts for referrals, monthly plans, or any other promotions that you've developed.

See chapter 3 for a description of how to set rates.

Scheduling

This tells clients how to obtain your services. Some cleaners set up a regular service schedule, while others ask their clients to confirm each appointment ahead of time. This section of your manual will outline your policy.

- Should regulars (say, once-a-week clients) confirm with you each week? Should clients call two weeks in advance of the intended day? Or should regular clients call only to change or cancel an appointment?
- How can the client reach you—phone, e-mail, beeper, or cell phone?
- Give a cut-off time for reservations (for example, by 8:00 p.m. Friday for the following week) or else you'll be bombarded with last-minute requests!

Cancellations

This will come to be of grave importance to you. There's nothing worse than having a client call and cancel two hours before a scheduled cleaning. You'll need a firm (very firm!) policy about how you will handle cancellations.

- You'll need to give clients a time period in which to cancel without penalty (for example, forty-eight hours in advance).
- Will you charge for cancellations with less than forty-eight hours' notice? If so, how much?
- What will happen if you wake up with the flu? Will you reschedule appointments for the following week? What about bimonthly clients—will they have to wait an entire month before services resume?
- Be sure to include a statement such as *Frequent cancellations may result in termination of services*. It gives you something to fall back on should you ever have to terminate a client who cancels services more often than she or he receives them.

Billing and Payments

As a professional service provider, you'll establish a method of billing. In this section, be specific as to when clients can expect their billing statements. Consider:

- Will you be billing on a weekly, biweekly, or monthly basis?
- How will the statements be sent: mailed, left at the residence, or e-mailed?

- What is the grace period between the statement date and the due date?
- What happens if payment is made late, or not at all?
- What payment options do you offer (credit card, check, money order)?
- Do you require a deposit from new clients?
- Do you offer bartering services? (This is a great way to give and get needed services!)
- What is the turnaround time for receipts? How and when should the client expect to receive her or his receipt?

We strongly recommend that you refrain from a cash-only policy. It gives an unprofessional impression. Also, as a sole proprietorship you are responsible for your own taxes. Dealing with cash is tricky; it's too easy to put it into your pocket, spend it, and not record it. Instead, you need to create a paper trail for each transaction. Insist on personal checks or credit cards (see chapter 2 for information on how to accept credit card payments). If clients must pay with cash, never allow them to leave it sitting unattended, such as on a kitchen counter. It's too easy for someone else to come along and take your money, and you have no proof that you didn't receive the cash. Save yourself the headache by insisting on checks and credit cards.

Contract Renewal

Don't forget to mention the dates of validity for the contract—is it good for a year, or six months? Include the date and year of expiration. Add a line or two to inform clients that they will be given ample time to read and review any changes or updates to the contract.

Community and Charitable Causes

Many business proprietors overlook the importance of charitable causes. Donating your services (offering to clean a church twice a year, for example) or sending a $10 check once a month to a community charity goes a long way. Make the contribution in the name of the business (it's tax deductible), and mention the charity here in a list of your contributions. Clients will appreciate the fact that you aren't all about the money.

General Information

Finally, you should include your insurance information: the name of the insurance company, your account number, and a toll-free number for clients to call and verify your coverage. Remember that you'll be handling the client's personal and prized belongings. Don't be insulted if someone does in fact call the insurance company. Also include the name and toll-free telephone number of your bonding company, and your bond certificate number. See chapter 12 for information on insurance and bonding.

It's a nice touch to include coupons for cleaning products. Be sure to check the expiration dates! You might also want to include business cards for other small businesses that offer services your clients may request: pet-sitting, yard tending, carpet cleaning, child care, errand services, and so forth. Once your business is established, you can network with many of these businesses for referrals.

Room Plans

At the back of the service manual, include a set of room plans. These are blank forms that you and the client can fill out together during the in-home consultation. They list exactly what tasks are to be performed in each room of the house. This lets the client know what services to expect, and it will help you develop the estimated time on tasks that enable you to set fees and schedules. Blank room plans are included in Appendix III, at the back of this book. You can adapt these forms to fit your own needs.

Sample Service Manual

Colonial Village Cleaners:
Guide to Services

123 Brownstone Street
Cleveland, Ohio 12345
(123) 555-1234
www.ColonialVillageCleaners.com
E-mail: Mjones@ColonialVillageCleaners.com
Serving the Suburban Cleveland Community

Thank you for inquiring about house- and apartment-cleaning services provided by Colonial Village Cleaners!

Mission Statement

Colonial Village Cleaners is a house- and apartment-cleaning service that has been providing professional cleaning to suburban Cleveland since November 2000. Our mission is to provide affordable, eco-friendly cleaning services so that people will not be overwhelmed with day-to-day household responsibilities.

Initial Contact

Prospective clients may either phone (123) 555-1234 or send an e-mail inquiry to Mjones@ColonialVillageCleaners.com. In return, a copy of the Guide to Services will be e-mailed as a Word document, or snail-mailed to an address that you specify. After reading our literature, you are encouraged to phone or e-mail with any questions or concerns. If you choose to hire our services, you should then call or e-mail to schedule a weekend appointment for an in-home consultation. Please note that all consultations are scheduled for either a Saturday or a Sunday.

The Consultation

Prospective clients and Mary Jones, the owner and service provider of Colonial Village Cleaners, and if applicable, an owner-assigned independent contractor, will meet at the client's home for a consultation that generally lasts between thirty and sixty minutes. During the consultation the following items will be discussed:

- We'll review your household needs as well as Colonial Village Cleaners' policies, service guide, payments, schedules, and any questions you might have.
- A sample home-cleaning plan, complete with room-by-room checklists, will be developed and available for your review within two business days. Once reviewed and approved, you and Mary Jones will sign the service contract and arrange a date for services to begin.
- Emergency information forms will be filled out.

A set of keys is to be provided to Mary Jones upon the signing of the service contract. Please note that we do not make secondary or follow-up visits to pick up or drop off keys or to pick up payments. If pickup or drop-off services are requested, you'll be charged the nominal hourly rate of $35 for each visit. You are more than welcome to make an appointment to pick up or drop off keys or payments at 123 Brownstone Street in Cleveland.

Please keep in mind that the consultation is a time for all parties to meet and share information regarding the servicing of the home. Not all cleaner-client matches are appropriate; therefore, we reserve the right to decline services.

Clientele

Colonial Village Cleaners provides house- and apartment-cleaning services to residents of suburban Cleveland. Approximately 70 percent of our client base consists of one-person households in which the resident works away from home an average of twelve hours per day, or sixty hours per week. The remaining 30 percent of our clients are families with multiple responsibilities: children, family activities, and involvement with community events.

Our Services

Visits are between two and four hours long, depending on the needs of your household. Colonial Village Cleaners will:

- give you a set time for your cleaning, with a one-hour variance to allow for traffic and road conditions;
- complete all services described in the home plan, and leave a completed plan on the dining room table or other designated area;
- provide its own cleaning products and tools, except as agreed upon according to your preferences;
- make suggestions with regard to cleaning products and procedures to ensure prompt and thorough cleaning of the household;
- dispose of chemicals in a utility or other sink that you designate;
- bring in mail and newspapers if asked to do so;

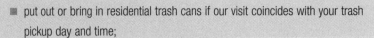

- put out or bring in residential trash cans if our visit coincides with your trash pickup day and time;

- send a monthly newsletter via e-mail (blind carbon copy) to inform clients of news, vacation dates, contests, and so forth; and

- maintain client house keys, home plans, and alarm codes in a fireproof safe at the residence of Mary Jones, proprietor.

Colonial Village Cleaners does not:

- provide service during the summer months to homes without adequate air-conditioning;

- provide service during the winter months to homes without adequate heating;

- provide service to households with unsupervised pets (please gate or crate your pet);

- provide service to households during the times that the house is occupied by unsupervised children or teenagers;

- provide services other than housecleaning (please feel free to inquire about referrals for vendors of other services);

- operate washing machines, dryers, stoves, trash compactors, or other electric, gas, or kerosene appliances;

- operate your motor vehicle;

- throw circuit breakers or replace fuses;

- let in service people such as water meter readers, UPS drivers, and so forth; or

- feed pets or clean up pet accidents.

We also do not:

- access your phone or answering machine;

- exchange keys with anyone other than the contracted client;

- use any chemical cleaning product not specified in writing; or

- sell or share residential or e-mail addresses, names, or telephone numbers with any other company or organization.

Hours of Operation

Colonial Village Cleaners generally provides services between 7:00 a.m. and 6:00 p.m., Monday through Friday. Business hours for voice mail are between 9:00 a.m. and 8:00 p.m., Monday through Friday; e-mail may be sent at any time. When phoning or e-mailing reservations, always wait for a confirmation. Our general response time is forty-eight hours.

Inclement Weather

Colonial Village Cleaners will provide limited, delayed, or no service during incidents of inclement weather:

- We will not provide mobile service during snow, sleet, ice, or hurricane-like weather. The only clients we service during extreme weather conditions are those within a safe walking distance from the residence of Mary Jones or the assigned independent contractor.

- Limited or delayed service may occur in extreme thunderstorms, in dangerously cold or hot conditions, and in any city- or state-declared weather emergency.

- All visits during a period of inclement weather will be on an hourly advisory status depending on the driving conditions.

Safety

Colonial Village Cleaners asks you to inform trustworthy neighbors, neighborhood watch organizations, relatives, and so forth that a housecleaner will be on your property. Doing so can save the police department, neighbors, and the housecleaner from an embarrassing situation.

Please notify Colonial Village Cleaners in advance (a few days is ideal) of any person or people who may be in your home during the time of the housecleaning service. This includes family members, service contractors, repair personnel, and so forth. Colonial Village Cleaners reserves the right to reschedule visits that coincide with a visit by another service contractor or houseguest.

Rates

- Initial consultations are free of charge.
- Each two-hour weekday visit to an apartment or house is $70.
- Each four-hour weekday visit to an apartment or house is $140.
- Each additional weekday hour beyond a four-hour visit is $35.
- Weekend visits are billed at the rate of $85 per two-hour visit.
- Colonial Village Cleaners offers a 10 percent discount to senior citizens and college students.

Reservations

To schedule a weekly visit, please phone or e-mail your reservation by 10:00 p.m. Friday for the following week. Please note that we do not use cell phones or beepers within the company. Always wait for a confirmation via e-mail or telephone. We can sometimes accommodate unplanned requests if we have a cancellation. However, we can rarely do so with less than twenty-four hours' notice.

Cancellations

- Please phone or e-mail (and wait for a confirmation) for all cancellations.
- Cancellations with less than forty-eight hours' notice (weekends and holidays included) are charged the nominal two-hour rate of $70. The only exception is inclement weather.
- Excessive cancellations with less than forty-eight hours' notice may lead to cessation of services. Please be sure of all dates and times when you e-mail or phone in your request. Calling to cancel on the morning of a

scheduled visit or two hours prior to the visit is inappropriate. We understand that emergencies arise, and that you may need to occasionally cancel services with less than forty-eight hours' notice. However, please reserve such cancellations for emergencies only.

Billing and Payments

A billing statement will be prepared every Monday and either e-mailed to you or left at your residence. Payment is expected within four days (weekends and holidays included).

Payment Options

- You may leave a check or money order at your residence on the day of the service. Please make all checks and money orders payable to Colonial Village Cleaners.

- Please do not postdate checks or money orders.

- You may mail a check or money order. Note that payments received after the due date are subject to late fees.

- You may pay with Visa, MasterCard, American Express, or Discover Card. We accept credit card payments through PayPal.com. Please ask for information on how to set up a free account with PayPal. PayPal is secure and encrypted.

- For security reasons, we do not accept cash left at residences. If you would like to pay in cash, please call or e-mail Mary Jones to arrange a drop-off time at 123 Brownstone Street.

- Occasionally we barter for services. If you have a professional service that you think may be of use to us, please feel free to ask! We've bartered services for graphic arts, pet-sitting, landscaping, and more. Bartering is one way that communities and small businesses can help each other.

Colonial Village Cleaners will issue a receipt within forty-eight hours after the payment is received. The receipt will be sent to you via e-mail or left at your residence. In some cases, a receipt may be snail-mailed to an address specified by the client.

Late Payments

Payments that are received beyond the due date listed on your billing statement are subject to late fees of $1.00 a day (weekends and holidays included) until the account is brought up to date. In cases of frequent late payments, Colonial Village Cleaners reserves the right to terminate services. Additional fees may be imposed for returned checks and closed accounts. In such cases, you will be charged $30 for each returned check (that's the service fee imposed on us by our bank), and any additional bank fees that are charged to us, as well as daily late fees that accrue until the account is brought up to date.

Referrals

Colonial Village Cleaners offers a 50 percent discount on a single four-hour visit for all completed referrals. This is our way of saying thanks to our wonderful and committed clients!

Below are two people who have given permission to be contacted for assignment-based references:
John Brown
123 Center Street
Cleveland, Ohio 12345
(123) 555-4444

Jane Doe
321 Round Street
Cleveland, Ohio 12345
(123) 555-2121

Contracts

Colonial Village Cleaners updates service guides and contracts on January 1 of each year. You will always receive a copy of the new contract in the month of

December. This gives you an opportunity to read and review the guide as well as to ask questions.

Community and Education

Colonial Village Cleaners provides some services free of charge to terminally ill Cleveland residents. Please ask for further information. We honor our commitment to helping community members in their times of need.

Colonial Village Cleaners is a member of the Cleveland Citizens Drug Awareness Program and is represented by Mary Jones, proprietor. We donate annually to the organization's fund to send disadvantaged children to summer camp. Mary Jones also sponsors and mentors a young person currently enrolled in the program.

General Information

Colonial Village Cleaners is insured and bonded by:
Generations Insurance Company of Ohio
P.O. Box 1234
Akron, Ohio 12345
(888) 555-5555
Account Number: 123-456-789

Colonial Village Cleaners is also bonded by:
Generations Insurance Company of Ohio
P.O. Box 5678
Akron, Ohio 12345
(888) 555-1111
Certificate Number: 789456
Colonial Village Cleaners is licensed as a service provider by the city of Cleveland. A copy of our business license is attached.

Home Plan

A home plan is a step-by-step guide for cleaning your home. We will review each room that you have requested to be cleaned, listing all required cleaning tasks for that room and which products will be used. We also include an estimated task time (ETT). This will give all parties an idea of the total amount of time necessary to complete a housecleaning. Estimated task times take into consideration:

- Cleaning behind heavy objects or several small objects that may need to be moved. An example might be removing a collection of glass jars from a tabletop, cleaning the jars as well as the tabletop, and returning the jars to the tabletop.

- Thorough indoor window cleaning: inside double-hung panes, as well the inward pane.

- Any buildup of kitchen grease, pet hair, hard water and lime stains, or wax residue.

- Intricate objects such as glass figurines or books that need to be removed, cleaned, and replaced.

Please understand that a thorough cleaning is a time-consuming process. We give added care and take precautions with furniture, collectibles, and other objects.

If you wish to make a change to the home plan after it has been completed and signed, please alert Mary Jones in writing, and allow two full weeks for a second draft to be drawn, reviewed, and signed, and for a copy to be provided to you.

Remember that making changes to a home plan means that the ETT will change. This may decrease or increase the time allotment necessary for service provision. We thus encourage you to carefully review your initial home plan. After the home plan has been accepted, please do not ask us to perform tasks that are not part of the contract. We will only provide the services included on the home plan.

Home Plan for John Burns, 456 Green Street

Client _____

Home telephone _____

Work telephone _____

Cell phone _____

E-mail address _____

Pets _____

_____

_____

Home alarm system _____ yes _____ no

Home alarm system code and instructions _____

_____

_____

Contact information for home alarm system provider _____

_____

_____

Dates valid _____ through _____

Emergency Information

Contact information for contractor or repair person _____

_____

_____

_____

Contact information for contractor or repair person _____

_____

_____

_____

Contact information for contractor or repair person _____

_____

_____

_____

Alternate Key Holders

Name _____

Address _____

_____

_____

Telephone _____

Cell phone _____

Relationship to client _____

Name _____

Address _____

_____

_____

Telephone _____

Cell phone _____

Relationship to client _____

Name _____

Address _____

_____

_____

Telephone _____

Cell phone _____

Relationship to client _____

Telephone and Account Numbers (where applicable)

Gas company _____

_____

_____

Electric company _____

_____

_____

Water bureau _____

_____

_____

_____

Telephone company _____

_____

_____

_____

Fire department _____

_____

_____

_____

Police department _____

_____

_____

_____

Poison control _____

_____

_____

_____

Room Plans

Client: John Burns   Room: Vestibule

Floor Finish

Wood _X_ Carpet ___ Tile ___ Other _____

1. Dry-mop.

2. Apply one coat of Seaside Naturals All Natural Hardwood Floor Cleaner.

Wall Finish

Wood paneling ___ Tile ___ Paint over plaster ___ Washable wallpaper over plaster ___ Wood wainscoting _X_ Plastic wainscoting ___ Other _____

1. Swipe with microfiber cloth.

2. Wipe down handprints and smudges with Begley's Best All Purpose Cleaner.

Entrance Door

Wood ___ Metal _X_

Door windows _X_

1. Metal door to be sprayed and wiped with Begley's Best All Purpose Cleaner.

2. Door windows to be sprayed with Bi-O-Kleen Glass Cleaner and wiped with a lint-free cloth.

3. Inside and outside doorknobs to be wiped with a lint-free cloth. No cleaning solvents to be used on the antique metal doorknobs or outside door knocker.

ETT: 20 minutes (Vestibule)

Client: John Burns   Room: Living Room

Floor Finish

Wood ____ Carpet _X_ Tile ____ Other _____

_____

1. Vacuum with freshening/deodorizing mixture of two parts baking soda, one part cornstarch.

Wall Finish

Wood paneling ___ Tile ___ Paint over plaster _X_ Washable wallpaper over plaster ___ Wood wainscoting _X_ Plastic wainscoting _____ Other _____

1. Swipe with microfiber cloth.

2. Handprints and smudges on wood wainscoting to be wiped down with Howard Naturals Wood Cleaner & Polish.

3. Painted wall surface to be wiped with lint-free cloth.

4. Wooden crevices can be blotted with a cloth and vinegar diluted with two parts water.

Appliances

Television _X_ VCR/DVD ___ Stereo component unit _X_ Humidifier _X_ Other _____

1. Television and stereo to be wiped down with Begley's Best All Purpose Cleaner and dry-wiped with microfiber cloth.

2. Humidifier to be cleaned externally with Bi-O-Kleen Glass Cleaner.

Other Furnishings

Coffee table _1_ Bookcase _4_ End table _2_ Paintings _2_ Floor lamps _1_ Table lamps _1_ Miscellaneous _____

_____

_____

_____

1. Two oil paintings on the wall to be lightly feather-dusted.

2. Books to be removed from bookcases and wiped with paper towel. Bookcase to be wiped down with Seaside Naturals Dusting Spray.

3. Metal lamp fixtures to be swiped with feather duster and glass portions wiped with Bi-O-Kleen Glass Cleaner.

4. Coffee table and end tables to be polished with Seaside Naturals Dusting Spray.

ETT: 30 minutes (Living Room)

Client: John Burns   Room: Kitchen

Floor Finish

Wood ___ Linoleum _X_ Tile ___ Other _____

1. Dry-mop.

2. Clean with Ecover Floor Soap.

Wall Finish

Wood paneling ___ Tile ___ Paint over plaster _X_ Washable
wallpaper over plaster _X_ Wood wainscoting ___ Plastic
wainscoting ____ Other _____

1. Swipe painted wall surface with microfiber cloth.

2. Wipe down wallpapered surface with damp cloth.

Countertop

Wood ____ Fiberglass ____ Tile _X_ Other _____
_____

1. Kitchen countertop to be wiped down with Begley's Best
All Purpose Cleaner and a damp sponge (*note that grout is
permanently stained).

Sink

Porcelain _X_ Acrylic ____ Stainless steel ____ Other _____
_____

1. Kitchen sink to be washed with Begley's Best All Purpose
Cleaner and a damp sponge—no abrasives (*note that the
kitchen's porcelain surface is scratched and permanently
stained).

2. Chrome fixtures to be cleaned with Bi-O-Kleen Glass Cleaner
and a damp sponge, and dried with a lint-free cloth.

Appliances

Stove _X_ Garbage disposal ___ Dishwasher ___ Refrigerator _X_
Trash compactor ____ Microwave oven _X_ Toaster oven _X_
Other _____

1. External surface of stove to be wiped with Seventh Generation Kitchen Cleaner (*note that around the burners is a heavy buildup of cooking deposits that cannot be removed by the housecleaner).

2. External surface of refrigerator to be wiped with Seventh Generation Kitchen Cleaner.

3. Microwave oven to be cleaned externally and internally with Begley's Best All Purpose Cleaner and damp sponge.

4. Toaster oven to be emptied of crumbs and cleaned externally with Begley's Best All Purpose Cleaner and damp sponge.

Miscellaneous Tasks

1. Plastic kitchen trash can to be soaked in Seventh Generation Kitchen Cleaner, rinsed, and wiped dry with reusable cloth.

2. Kitchen trash to be placed in trash bin outdoors.

3. Collection of ceramic cookie jars to be cleaned with Begley's Best All Purpose Cleaner.

4. Wooden cabinets to be wiped with Howard Naturals Wood Cleaner & Polish and damp sponge.

5. Small kitchen window to be cleaned (inside only) with Bi-O-Kleen Glass Cleaner and reusable cloth.

ETT: 30 minutes (Kitchen)

Client: John Burns   Room: Bathroom

Floor

Laminate _X_ Tile ____ Marble ____ Other _____

_____

1. Floor to be dry-mopped and wet-mopped with Ecover Floor Soap.

Tub/Shower

Fiberglass _X_ Porcelain ____ Ceramic tile ____ Other _____

chrome fixtures _____

_____

1. Tub and shower unit to be cleaned with Naturally Yours Basin, Tub & Tile Cleaner and rinsed clean.

2. Chrome fixtures to be cleaned with Mrs. Meyer's premoistened surface wipes.

Toilet

1. Toilet bowl to be cleaned with Seventh Generation Natural Mint Toilet Cleaner and brush.

2. Toilet surfaces to be cleaned with Begley's Best All Purpose Cleaner and wiped with lint-free soft cloth.

Walls

Wooden wainscoting _X_ Painted plaster _X_ Tile ____ Other __

_____

1. Wooden wainscoting to be wiped free of smudges and fingerprints with Howard Naturals Wood Cleaner & Polish and a damp cloth.

2. Painted plaster walls to be wiped with Begley's Best All Purpose Cleaner and damp reusable cloth.

Vanity

Porcelain _X_ Stainless steel ___ Acrylic ___ Formica _X_ Wood ____ Glass _X_ Chrome _X_ Other _glass vases_____

1. Formica vanity to be wiped with Begley's Best All Purpose Cleaner and microfiber cloth.

2. Porcelain sink to be cleaned with Naturally Yours Basin, Tub & Tile Cleaner and wiped with lint-free soft cloth.

3. Chrome fixtures to be cleaned with Mrs. Meyer's premoistened surface wipes.

4. Mirror above vanity to be cleaned with Bi-O-Kleen Glass Cleaner and reusable cloth.

5. Glass vases on vanity to be wiped with microfiber cloth.

Door

Wood _X_ Glass _X_ Other _____

1. Wooden door to be dusted with feather duster, then damp-wiped with Howard Naturals Wood Cleaner & Polish and damp sponge.

2. Glass mirror on door's inside to be cleaned with Bi-O-Kleen Glass Cleaner and lint-free paper towel.

Towel Rack and Wall Decorations

Chrome _____ Wood _X_ Acrylic _____ Glass _X_ Other _____

_____

1. Wooden towel rack to be cleaned with microfiber cloth.

2. Three wooden picture frames to be cleaned with microfiber cloth.

3. Glass on picture frames to be cleaned with Bi-O-Kleen Glass Cleaner and reusable cloth.

ETT: 30 minutes (Bathroom)

Client: John Burns   Room: Bedroom 1

Floor

Carpet _X_ Wood _X_ Tile ____ Other _____

1. Carpet to be vacuumed with freshening/deodorizing mixture of two parts baking soda, one part cornstarch.

2. Wood portions to be dry-mopped then lightly mopped with Seaside Naturals All Natural Hardwood Floor Cleaner and damp sponge mop.

Nightstand and Dresser

Wood _X_ Glass____ Acrylic _X_ Other _____

1. Wooden nightstand to be cleaned with Pledge brand wood cleaner and lint-free paper towel.

2. Dresser to be cleaned with Howard Naturals Wood Cleaner & Polish after decorative acrylic items are removed.

3. Decorative acrylic items to be cleaned with Begley's Best All Purpose Cleaner and soft reusable cloth.

ETT: 30 minutes (Bedroom 1)

Client: John Burns   Room: Laundry Room

Metal Appliances

Washer _X_ Dryer _X_

1. Washer and dryer to be cleaned with Begley's Best All Purpose Cleaner.

Utility Sink

Acrylic ____ Stainless steel _X_ Other _____

1. Acrylic utility sink to be cleaned out with Howard Naturals Stainless Steel Cleaner & Polish and wiped with reusable cloth.

ETT: 10 minutes (Laundry Room)

Home Plan: John Burns, 456 Green Street

Vestibule: 20 minutes

Living Room: 30 minutes

Kitchen: 30 minutes

Bathroom: 30 minutes

Bedroom 1: 30 minutes

Laundry Room: 10 minutes

Total time: 2 hours 30 minutes

Charge: $87.50

I have read the service guide and agree to the home plan that has been supplied to me by Mary Jones of Colonial Village Cleaners. I agree to the policies as described in the manual, as well as to the customized home plan that has been developed for me.

_____

(Client Signature)

_____

 (Date)

_____

Mary Jones, Colonial Village Cleaners

_____

(Date)

05

How to Screen Clients

Not all cleaner-client matches are ideal. That's why screening your clients is so important. If you do a careful job of screening and keep an eye out for potential problems, you and your clients will both be happy.

By Telephone

The phone rings—and there's a potential client on the other end! It's human nature to stutter and forget your memorized speech. It's good to remember that almost no one notices nervousness. It will also help if you write your greeting spiel down on an index card that you keep by the telephone. If you get nervous, you can refer to it.

The first question a client usually asks is "What are your rates?" Head off this question by asking if she or he has received your Guide to Services. Take a few minutes to explain your policy of sending this guide to the client for review, and that the next step is to schedule an in-home consultation. Never quote prices or give estimates over the telephone, no matter how insistent the caller is. You have more to offer than just a price, and you want to make sure callers understand everything your business can do for them.

You should also use this time to ask the client where she or he lives. If it's an area that's not in your zone, you've already saved yourself time and trouble. Be sure to refer the caller to a cleaner who does service the area.

If the caller has already received the Guide to Services and is phoning to schedule a consultation, congratulations! This means that the client has read the information, finds it acceptable, and is ready to meet you. Ask if you can answer any questions, and reiterate that the purpose of the consultation is to produce an initial home plan. When making arrangements for an in-home consultation, be sure to get detailed directions to the client's home.

Regardless of the directions the client gives, check out a city map, or go to one of the free online map services such as MapQuest (www.mapquest.com) or Yahoo! Maps (http://maps.yahoo.com) and download a copy of the directions. Having a map will allow you to choose an alternate route in case of unexpected road construction or detours.

Be safety-conscious when agreeing to meet a stranger. Tell a family member or a friend where you're going and when you expect to return. If anything sounds suspicious about the caller, mention that you'll be bringing a companion. Still, if you're not sure about the integrity of the caller, it's better not to take a chance. Sometimes callers sound strange because they're uncomfortable talking on the phone, or they aren't sure what to say or ask. Use your best judgment. If something doesn't seem quite right, it probably isn't.

Don't forget to ask the client about household pets. It would not serve you well to be greeted at the front door by a German shepherd if you're afraid of or allergic to dogs.

Ask the client where she or he heard about your services: Web site, business card, or referral? This is great feedback for your marketing strategy. If you printed 200 flyers, tacked them to bulletin boards, and left them at various establishments—and none of your callers mentions the flyer—then you've learned how *not* to advertise.

In Person

Carry a service bag that will hold extra copies of your Guide to Services, information forms, business cards, and blank room plans, as well as a map, clipboard, notebook, small stapler, pens, and pencils. Keep everything labeled and organized so you don't have to fumble. When you greet the client, be sure to give a firm handshake. This shows confidence and respect. Explain to the client that the consultation process generally takes an hour, or whatever time limit you've specified in your manual. Ask the client to give you a tour of the home. For each room that you're shown, take a room-plan sheet and fill out the header to indicate the room. It should take fifteen minutes or so to do an initial tour. Don't worry about writing down anything yet; you'll be doing a second walk-through.

When the initial tour is completed, you and the client will go through each room a second time. During the second walk-through, the client identifies the specific services requested. Use this time to clarify services and requests as well as the products to be used.

Red Flags

Here are some danger signals to keep in the back of your mind as you talk to potential clients. Any of the following red flags may indicate a problem or the potential for one:

- Racist or sexist comments or jokes.

- Comments or jokes that demean you or any service professionals.

- Clients who pump you for personal information—or, conversely, those who offer too much info about themselves. In other words, you want to be careful around folks who seem to overstep the limits of a client–service provider relationship.

- Clients with unreasonable expectations of your time and services.

- Clients who obviously cannot afford your services.

- A home in unacceptably filthy condition.

- A home that presents possible safety issues—rickety stairways, leaky plumbing or gas pipes, blatant insect or rodent infestation, and so on.

- The potential for unsupervised children or pets being on the property while you clean—especially if the client seems unresponsive to your concerns about them.

- A home whose layout or contents may be beyond your capacities as a housecleaner. Some houses require expertise or agility that's simply not among your gifts. There's no shame in admitting it.

- A home that presents travel obstacles—maybe it's just a long way outside your usual geographic territory, or perhaps the driveway is too steep for anything but four-wheel-drive vehicles.

- It's tempting to take on new clients despite serious reservations, especially when you're just starting out. That's one reason to build waiting periods into your client-screening procedure. Use them. Think carefully about your doubts and determine how you'd like to proceed. The longer you're in this business, the more finely tuned your instincts will become for possible problems. Also see chapter 14, "When Bad Things Happen to Good Housecleaners," for more on uncomfortable people situations.

Here are some things to keep in mind:

- Point out and ask about furniture or fixtures that the client didn't specify. During the second walk-through, for instance, you might notice a mirror behind the bathroom door that the client didn't mention. Is this to be cleaned as well?
- Ask about the handling of fragile or decorative items. Use your judgment with fragile items. If you don't feel comfortable being asked to clean an original Tiffany lamp, say so!
- Ask about household pets. If there's a dog, where will it be while you're working in the home? Are there any exotic family pets that you need to know about—say, boa constrictors caged in the basement, or a tarantula kept under a teenager's bed?
- Ask who will be in the home when you are cleaning: unsupervised children, a grandmother, another service provider? Be cautious here. You don't want to sound suspicious of the client's household members, but you are entitled to work in peace and comfort, without feeling as though someone's watching you. You dictate what's comfortable for you.
- Avoid making any sort of commitment to the assignment, dates, or times. Review with the client how the estimate process works. You'll take the written information and draw up an estimate that includes a total ETT, rate, and schedule of availability. The client will receive a copy and will have a few days to verify the estimate. Inevitably, a client will have forgotten a task or will want to remove one. This means that you need to reevaluate the home plan. It may take a week or so before you can negotiate a complete home plan. Still, it's better to take the extra week now than to get halfway through a daily assignment only to have the client add or remove a task.
- You are interviewing the client as much as the client is interviewing you. If anything about the client or the home makes you feel uncomfortable, speed up the consultation process, thank the client, say you'll be in touch, and get out. See the sidebar "Red Flags" for some of the warning signs to look for.

Just Say No

For a lot of us, that little two-letter word, *no,* can sure be complicated! Once you're in business for yourself, however, no is your best friend. Sooner or later in your housecleaning career, you'll be asked to give an estimate for a home or client that makes you uncomfortable. (For any number of reasons—see the "Red Flags" sidebar.) So how do you turn down an assignment with dignity and professionalism intact?

The Victorian Butler

In the late nineteenth century, a butler's duties ranged from maintaining and accounting for the household's china, silver, glassware, and linens to answering the door for callers. The butler also held the keys to the wine cellar, where his responsibilities included decanting wines and choosing the correct vintage to complement each meal. Depending on the household, the butler was also known to brew beer. He assisted at meals by pouring coffee or tea for breakfast and by pouring wine for dinner. During the meals, when he wasn't pouring, the butler stood behind the master's chair.

While you're still in the client's home, smile, and treat the client with courtesy and respect. If you know you'll be turning this assignment down (and sometimes you know instantly), get out as soon as you comfortably can. It's fine to use a white lie ("Oh my goodness, look at the time!") if this is easier for you. If you're unsure of your final decision, however—and you feel that the situation is safe—continue with your interview carefully. Be as noncommittal as possible. Once you leave the interview—wait. The client-screening process we've described in this chapter includes built-in waiting periods. Outside the potential client's presence and home, you'll be able to think far more thoroughly and clearly about your reservations and about how you want to proceed. When you need to say no, the easiest way to do so is in writing. Send the potential client a note. Snail mail is more detached and aloof than e-mail, which is probably what you want. You can lay out the reasons behind your refusal if you're comfortable with this, but again, it's fine to use a white lie: "I've realized I'm simply more swamped than I'd thought" offends no one.

Follow Through

Once you've left the client's home, be sure to follow through with providing the estimate by the stated date. If your estimate is late, you're sending the message that you have difficulties with promptness, and that's not a great first impression. If you don't hear from the client within a day or two of dropping off the estimate, give a call. If changes need to be made, do so immediately, and get the corrected copy to the client within two business days of the requested change. If the prospective client agrees to the services you've outlined, celebrate—but also think about committing yourself to two cleanings only; at that point, you and the client can both have a chance to reevaluate things and make sure the match is right. This gives you an easy way out of a contract if anything about the assignment turns out to make you uncomfortable.

Now it's time to roll up your sleeves and go to work!

06

Cleaning 101

Yes, you've cleaned before. But do you know how to clean in the most efficient, stress-free way possible? How to shop for supplies and take care of your aching back? As you embark on your new career, you'll quickly develop cleaning methods that work for you. Here are a few tips and tricks to help get you started in the right direction.

The Well-Stocked Cleaner

First of all, you've got a decision to make: Do you want to use your clients' cleaning supplies and equipment, or do you want to bring your own? If you're just starting out and short on cash, using clients' products could be the way to go. It doesn't involve any cash outlay for you, and you don't have to worry about clients not liking your products. In addition, you'll save yourself the aches and pains of lugging bottles and jars in and out of your clients' homes.

Still, bringing your own supplies has a lot of advantages. These include:

- You can stick with the products that work best for you, saving time and energy when you clean.
- You don't have to worry that your clients will run out of the products you need.
- You can organize your products in a caddy and/or cleaning apron that you bring with you on every job. You'll know exactly where everything is all the time, and you'll save time (and footsteps!) by having it at your side.
- You know exactly how to use each product, and what it's best for.

- Ecologically friendly, hypoallergenic, scent-free, and super-strength products are all available, and offering these to your clients can be a strong selling point for your business.
- You'll simply project a sharper, more businesslike, more professional image.

Of course, if a client prefers a certain product, good customer service dictates that you use it.

There are countless cleaning products on the market, and you'll want to do some experimenting to see what you like. It's easiest to buy your products from a retail outlet: grocery stores, discount houses, and drugstores all stock good brands. Do some comparison shopping, however. Janitorial supply firms and many companies on the Internet offer specialized products that might be much better suited to your needs. You can also find concentrates that allow you to mix your own cleaning solutions in spray bottles; these save money and packaging. The busier you are, the more it's worth taking the time to find products you can really trust.

What does a well-supplied housecleaner need? Here's a list of some essentials that you can start with. Of course, you'll want to tailor it to fit your own and your clients' needs.

- Cleaning caddy. This is a fantastic time saver! Make sure it's deep enough to prevent products from tipping over. Look for a comfortable carrying handle, too.
- Cleaning apron. You can carry many supplies and products right on your person if you have a cleaning apron with lots of pockets and hooks. Cloths, towels, brushes, spray bottles, and more can all be kept here. You can even make or adapt your own cleaning apron for maximum efficiency. Use a sturdy, easy-care fabric. You may want to have a spare or two in case an apron is drenched, stained, ripped, or otherwise damaged on the job. PS: Some cleaners replace aprons with fanny packs. It's your call!
- Stain-removal options. See page 87 for "Your Stain-Removal Toolbox," a list of stain-removing treatments you might like to have handy.
- Mild all-purpose cleaner for countertops, faucets, cabinets, and the like. Spray bottles are handiest.
- Disinfectant cleaner for bathroom and kitchen cleaning. Again, use a spray bottle.

- Abrasive cleaner, but not too abrasive. A mild formulation won't damage surfaces.
- Glass cleaner for glass, mirrors, TVs, and shiny black appliances.
- General wood cleaner for wooden floors, cupboards, wainscoting, baseboards, and other wood surfaces.
- Brushes and/or scrub pads. You can either choose a utility brush and a mini brush (soft bristles will prevent scratches), or use nylon scrubbing pads.
- Feather or lamb's-wool duster.
- Cleaning cloths. Microfiber is the new rage in cleaning products, and it's great stuff: Millions of tiny fibers trap dust and dirt, making cleaning efficient and easy. You can wash and reuse the cloths, too. Also look for lint-free paper towels.
- Dust formula. Apply this to your cleaning cloths and your dry mop.
- Dry mop. These are generally much better than brooms for initial floor cleanup. A broom just moves the dirt around the floor, but dirt and dust particles will cling to a dry mop.
- Wet mop and mop bucket. Some cleaners swear by sponge mops, others by string heads. See what works best for you. In general, the sponge types are more convenient for small areas, string mops for larger floors.
- Squeegees can give you great results on glass, tile, and porcelain.
- Gloves. If your hands are sensitive, these can be lifesavers.

Cleaners have reported carrying a huge variety of other assorted tools and oddments for those tricky, painful, or obscure cleaning problems. Think about: Q-tips, old toothbrushes, knee pads, and/or a lint roller. Think about anything else that works, too!

A Cleaning Play-by-Play

Cleaning technique is, of course, a very individual matter. Everyone cleans a little differently, and there is really no right or wrong way. Still, there are a few tricks of the trade that might help you out, or at least give you something to think about. Chances are you'll agree with some and disagree intensely with others. That's fine! The right method is the one that works best for you.

Most cleaners would agree, however, that in this business, time is money. The more quickly you can clean a house—without sacrificing thoroughness—the more

Choosing a Vacuum

Investing in a top-notch vacuum cleaner may be one of the wisest moves you can make. Yes, they're expensive: hundreds of dollars for the best quality. And you might not be able to afford one right away. But a good vacuum will save you a lot of time and energy; you'll get the same results (or better) with far less work. The best vacuums allow you to offer clients a level of cleaning they'll never achieve on their own. That's a strong selling point for your services!

When you are ready to make the investment, here are some things to consider as you decide on which vacuum is right for you:

- **Type.** Upright or canister? Uprights work well on wall-to-wall carpeting, but they don't reach under furniture. Canisters work well on all kinds of surfaces, are much more flexible, and are generally a better bet for the housecleaner.

- **Airflow.** Measured in cfm (cubic feet per minute), this is the real indicator of a vacuum's efficiency. It tells you how much suction power the machine has. The higher, the better.

- **Amps.** A high-amp vacuum is not necessarily a stronger one; it just uses more electricity. Airflow is a more important characteristic to look for in judging vacuums.

- **Attachments.** Does the model have the attachments you need? Can you add new attachments later as your needs change?

- **Cost and ease of maintenance.** What will you have to pay for replacement bags, belts, and filters? Are they readily available? What about repairs—are there good repair resources at a convenient distance from you, and are they affordable?

- **Filtration quality.** Some canister-type vacuums can filter out allergenic particles; this might be important to some of your clients. Look for HEPA (high-efficiency particulate air) or ULPA (ultra low penetration air) filters if any of your clients suffer from respiratory or other allergy problems. These vacuums are, of course, more expensive.

jobs you can fit into a day, and the more money you can earn. If you can complete the basics more quickly, you'll also have time to offer clients little extra touches that will keep them coming back. So how can you be most efficient? Here are some tips:

- Make the most of every movement. You can save an amazing amount of time by simply paying a little attention to your movements. You want to avoid backtracking: Remember, each footstep spent retrieving the can of cleanser you left in another room costs you time and energy.
- Where do you start cleaning? Naturally, you don't want to be tracking new dirt into rooms you've already cleaned, so it's most efficient to start with the least central rooms: usually bathrooms and bedrooms. Save the kitchen and other high-traffic areas for last
- Work around a room in a circle, clockwise or counterclockwise, whatever works best for you. You'll minimize footsteps and be less likely to leave any tasks out.
- Work from top to bottom. You don't want to re-clean surfaces that your cleaning process itself messed up.
- Clean dry, then clean wet. You want to remove dirt and dust before applying any cleaning solution.
- Let your products work for you. After you apply a cleaning solution, give it a few minutes to work before rinsing it off.
- Have the supplies you need at hand. It's best to carry them with you in a caddy or your cleaning apron.

- Keep tools and equipment in good working order. Rinse your brushes at the end of a job. Throw cleaning cloths into the washing machine at the end of the day; do the same with dust mops periodically. Change your vacuum cleaner bags and filters regularly.

Bathroom

- Clean the tub/shower from top to bottom with an all-purpose or disinfectant cleaner; be careful to use nothing abrasive on fiberglass. Ceramic tile may call for a scrubbing brush or pad. (Be careful not to scrub too hard.) Glass shower doors can be cleaned with glass cleaner. Don't forget to check the door runners and clean with a brush and paper towels if needed. It's a good idea to put a cloth or paper towels down on the floor; you can stand on these while you clean to avoid tracking dirt into the tub.
- Clean the toilet bowl first with disinfectant or toilet bowl cleaner; let the cleaner do its work for a few minutes, then brush and flush. Next, clean the seat and other surfaces by spraying with disinfectant cleaner, letting it stand, and wiping with a cloth or paper towels.
- Wipe the walls and light switches.
- Spray the countertop with disinfectant or all-purpose cleaner and wipe it dry.
- Clean the sink and faucets with disinfectant or all-purpose cleaner and wipe dry.
- As a final touch, try spraying the counter and sinks with Pledge and wiping dry.
- Cleaning the soap dish is another extra touch that bigger cleaning companies don't do but clients appreciate.
- Clean the mirror with glass cleaner and lint-free paper towels.
- Finally, dry-mop the floor, then wet-mop or wax it.

Living Room, Bedrooms, and Similar Areas

Living rooms, family rooms, dens, offices, bedrooms . . . all these rooms involve the same sorts of cleaning tasks. Some cleaners dust and swipe before they vacuum (on the theory that the dust will fall to the floor, where it can then be vacuumed away); others vacuum before they dust (because the vacuum stirs up dust in the room, which the dusting will then take away). If your vacuum is top-notch, you'll probably want to at least give the dust-first method a try. If you're using an older model (or a client's older model), it's worth keeping the vacuum-first method in mind. As always, the right method is whatever works best for you.

- When you dust, move around the room, starting high and moving down. Paintings and bookshelves might come first, for instance, followed by table-tops.
- Anytime you use dust formula, apply it to your cloth, not to the surface you're cleaning.
- A TV screen can be gone over with an electrostatic cloth. You can also spray glass cleaner onto a cleaning cloth (never onto the screen), wipe the screen, then dry it.
- Don't forget to give electrical switchplates a once-over. They're inevitably covered with fingerprints.
- It's better to vacuum slowly and thoroughly than to go over the same floor again and again.
- Vacuum systematically. It can be helpful to divide a large room into sections and move from one to the next. Be sure your system doesn't require you to walk over just-vacuumed areas.

Stairways

Wooden stairs can be dry-mopped. Work from the top down.

Carpeted stairs can be vacuumed with an upright vacuum; working from the top down may be easier on your back. You might prefer to do this job with a canister vacuum, however, or with a mini vac. Whatever you do, be careful not to let the cord get in the way.

Kitchen

The order in which you clean the kitchen will be determined by its floor plan. As always, work around the room, from top to bottom.

- Clean any countertop appliances: Remove crumbs from the toaster oven and clean it; clean the microwave inside and out. (Specialized cleaners are available for this, or you can use a mild all-purpose cleaner.)

- Clean the countertops with an all-purpose or disinfectant cleaner. Remember to move appliances out of the way and clean underneath them as well.
- Clean the stovetop with an all-purpose or disinfectant cleaner.
- Wipe down the refrigerator, oven, dishwasher, washing machine, and dryer with all-purpose or glass cleaner.
- Clean the sink with a nonabrasive all-purpose or disinfectant cleaner, or a specialized cleaner for the particular surface. Let the cleaner sit for a few minutes before rinsing; then wipe the sink dry with a lint-free cloth or paper towel.
- Finally, dry-mop the floor, then wet-mop or wax it.

Stains

As a professional housecleaner, stains are your life: cleaning them and (even more so) dispensing guidance on how to clean them. Below are some tips to get you started; you will quickly develop your own repertoire of stain secrets.

Stains 1: Stuff that Stains

Be prepared to deal with stains from the organic (grass, mud) to the biological (pet hair and urine, dead insects), the luxe (wine, chocolate, caviar) to the just plain strange (melted guitar picks?). As a general rule, the faster you can treat a stain, the better. You'll rarely have the luxury of being present when a stain is created, though, so the following stain information is divided into two categories: advice (what to tell your clients about immediate stain treatment) and action (what to do about those long-term stains you'll actually be greeted with at clients' homes).

Coffee Stains

Advice: Rinse or blot immediately with cool water.

Action: If this doesn't work, try diluted detergent (with a few drops of vinegar for extra strength) or hydrogen peroxide.

Cosmetics Stains

Advice: Tell your clients to start by applying nail polish remover or rubbing with bar soap.

Action: Next on the agenda: diluted detergent, diluted vinegar, and commercial spot removers.

Grease and Oil Stains

Advice: Start by dabbing with a paper towel, then applying nail polish remover (unless the fabric or carpet is made of acetate). You can also try treating the spill with an absorbent powder, such as talcum powder or cornstarch. This will help absorb the grease.

Action: Try treating with a commercial spot remover, petroleum jelly, or a commercial oil solvent.

Ink Stains

Advice: Ink is a real bear to remove. For ballpoint ink, try rubbing alcohol or a mixture of water, detergent, and ammonia. For felt-tip ink, an all-purpose cleaner is your first resort.

Action: Your last resort is to continue treatment with the materials noted above. Another possibility is diluted bleach—although this can, as you might expect, bleach the material.

Pet Stains

Advice: Hair, urine, vomit, and um, other substances: Pets (bless their hearts) love to leave us "gifts." Hair can be removed (in the short- or the long-term) with a vacuum (regular or handheld), a lint brush or pet-grooming brush, or the sticky side of some wide tape (packing tape or duct tape, perhaps). Urine should be treated as quickly as possible: First blot it up with a white paper towel. Then try applying diluted detergent or diluted vinegar, covering the area with a towel and something heavy, and letting it dry. A final suggestion, and maybe the best one for pet owners: All kinds of enzyme-based products are now specifically made for cleaning urine. They work.

Feces and spit-up should be immediately removed (your clients will, hopefully, perform this step as quickly as humanly possible). Then diluted detergent can be blotted on. Commercially available odor removers will help, too.

Action: If you come across a stain that's set in for a while, the treatments described above are your best bet. Try applying treatment as early in your cleaning day as possible, then returning to it just before you leave to see how it's worked. If you have a lot of pet-owning clients, it's smart to carry special brushes, enzyme-based cleaners, and odor removers right in your cleaning caddy or vehicle.

Red Wine Stains

Advice: Fast action is crucial. If they can, your clients should immediately use a cloth or noncolored paper towel to apply white wine to a red wine stain. (Don't rub, just blot.) Other stain removers to try include club soda (apply just like the white wine), salt (this keeps the stain from setting, at least for a little while), and plain old water (again, blot on with a cloth or white paper towel).

Action: Be prepared with some bad news for your client. If a red wine stain has set into fabric or carpet, it may be permanent. Before abandoning all hope, though, you can try carpet shampoo or one of the many commercial carpet or fabric cleaners, including some made specifically for wine stains.

Water Stains

Advice: Yes, water is what's supposed to fix stains, not cause them. Nevertheless, it can be a problem, particularly on wood. Advising clients on watermarks is easy: Because those marks can fade on their own, the first course of action is to wait a few days.

Action: So your clients waited, and the stain is still there? Try rubbing the watermark with a gentle abrasive (nothing too coarse, and not too much elbow grease). Extra-fine steel wool or cheesecloth might work. You can try mineral spirits or a lubricant such as paste wax or diluted household ammonia. Rub with the wood grain, not against it.

Your Stain-Removal Toolbox

It's a good idea to have some stain-removing treatments close at hand as you travel from appointment to appointment—a little insurance for the problems sure to confront you. Think about keeping a separate kit specifically for stains. You probably don't need all these materials in your regular caddy or apron, but you might like to have them at hand in your vehicle:

- ammonia
- baking soda
- chlorine bleach
- club soda
- commercial stain removers (experiment with these and find a repertoire of products you can depend on)
- cornstarch
- dry-cleaning solvent
- enzyme-based pet-urine cleaner
- hydrogen peroxide
- mild detergent
- odor remover
- oil solvent
- petroleum jelly
- rubbing alcohol
- white vinegar

You can find myriad stain-removing commercial products on the market—more and more all the time—and some really are effective. Experiment with these (be careful with your lungs, your fabrics, and your pocketbook) and see what works for you. And prepare an I-have-bad-news-for-you speech for your clients for those stains that are immortal.

Stains II: Stuff that Gets Stained

Clients will decorate their homes with almost anything—from concrete to marble, silk to wicker. Some of these fabrics and substances naturally require extra care. The more you know about special treatments for special materials, the better you can serve your customers. Doing a bit of homework on the stuff of your clients' lives can pay off (see "Stains III: Stuff that Talks about Stains" for where to start your research). In the meantime, here are some of the biggies:

Brick

Sweep or vacuum, damp-mop with plain water, or mop with an alkali solution.

Hardwood

Vacuum or sweep. Talk to your clients about their specific type of floor and finish (polyurethane, shellac, varnish, wax); different kinds require different products. If possible, follow the floor manufacturer's recommendations. If clients don't know the specifics of their floor, try a general wood cleaner.

Ceramic Tile

The main problem with ceramic is its grout. And clients will love you if you can keep their grout sparkling. Clean it regularly with a gentle bathroom cleanser, diluted bleach, or (for white grout only) diluted hydrogen peroxide, as well as a brush. Don't scrub too hard or use abrasives—this can damage the grout.

Concrete

Sweep; mop with diluted detergent or with trisodium phosphate (this can be dangerous, so read and follow all the label instructions). You may have to scrub.

Glass

You may or may not "do windows" (that choice is entirely yours!). Even if you don't, however, many homes have glass tabletops or other glass features, and virtually all of 'em have mirrors. So it's worth knowing how to make glass sparkle. Use diluted detergent or diluted vinegar, then wipe dry; a squeegee is best for windows, but other glass fixtures might require newsprint or a chamois cloth. And when applicable, remember to clean both sides of the glass.

Marble

You'd think that stone would be tough, but marble is in fact a very delicate material. Never use products that contain acid or abrasives. For regular cleaning, use an untreated dust mop, or damp-mop with diluted detergent. When you're done, dry the marble with a towel. Recommend to your clients that they have the marble sealed—this will prolong its life and make cleaning a lot easier.

Porcelain

Sinks, tubs, toilets, and more are often made of porcelain. For regular cleaning, use a general household cleaner, diluted baking soda, or a nonabrasive bathroom cleaner. Avoid harsh products and harsh scrubbing; porcelain can be a bit sensitive.

Stone

Use a dust cloth or, for floors, a dust mop or vacuum. Then damp-clean with a cleaner created specifically for stone.

Vinyl and Linoleum

Sweep, vacuum, or dust-mop, then damp-mop with a no-rinse cleaner. If the flooring has grown dull, try an acrylic floor polish (apply lightly).

Stains III: Stuff that Talks about Stains

Everyone and her brother has something to say about stain treatment, so there are any number of other resources you can turn to for further information. Be wary: Selling "miracle" stain removers (at exorbitant prices) is one of the oldest con games out there. Still, there are some excellent products and suggestions available.

For starters, you can simply type "stain removal" into any Internet search engine and settle in for a long, long read. Here are some specific sites you might want to try:

- www.pioneerthinking.com/cleaningsolutions.html. Click on the specific stain you're trying to remove under "Stain Removers."
- http://doityourself.com. Click "Household and Cleaning." DoItYourself.com offers general cleaning information—and a lot more.
- www.butlersguild.com/index.php?subject=152. Offered by the International Guild of Professional Butlers.
- http://housekeeping.about.com/od/stainremoval/a/stainsindex.htm. Part of About.com, a huge Web resource packed with information about, well, everything.

A Green Stain-Removal Kit

Green doesn't have to mean stained. If you're going green (see chapter 7), you'll still want an arsenal of natural, chemical-free, earth-friendly remedies that help you get spots out. Here's a good beginner's kit of various kinder, gentler products and substances that are still tough on dirt:

- **Water.** Yep, this is the first line of defense. Cold water and a couple of towels start any stain-removal process. Boiling water is good for red wine stains.

- **Castile soap** is made from vegetable oil; it's the mildest out there. Check out the products available from Dr. Bronner's Magic Soaps.

- **White distilled vinegar** works miracles in any number of cleaning applications, including stain removal. It's inexpensive and available everywhere to boot. Have some with you at all times.

- **Cornstarch** is good on grease and protein stains, and can help freshen and deodorize a room. (Protein stains include any number of biological substances, from foods—think eggs and milk—to feces.)

- **Baking soda** is also good on grease. Combine it with cornstarch (2 parts soda to 1 part cornstarch), sprinkle it on carpets, let it sit for several hours, and then vacuum for a natural carpet freshener and deodorizer. Add essential oils to the mixture for a lovely scent.

- **Enzyme soaks,** such as Bi-O-Kleen's Bac-Out Stain & Odor Eliminator, also work on protein stains.

- **Club soda** works well on rugs.

- **Lemon juice** is useful on wine stains as well as rust and hard-water deposits.

- **Milk** is helpful on ink stains.

- **Hydrogen peroxide** treats mustard stains as well as cosmetics stains. Caution: It does tend to lighten fabrics.

As with all stain-removal products, test your product of choice on a small bit of the stain before using it on the entire area. While green stain removers are less problematic to mix than many chemical counterparts, do be careful about combining them.

- For carpet stains: www.a2zcarpet.com. Click on "Stain Removal Guide." This site offers myriad resources for both consumers and carpet-cleaning pros.
- For fabric stains: www.fabriclink.com/holidaystain.html. Info and resources for fabric professionals and just plain folks.
- For eco-friendly stain removal tips: www.davidsuzuki.org/files/NC/newsletter/stainremoval.pdf.

You can find stain removal information in any number of books, too—you can even carry a written guide in your cleaning caddy or your vehicle for quick reference. The following volumes are organized alphabetically to help you get at the info you need, fast:

- *The Cleaning Encyclopedia: Your A to Z Illustrated Guide to Cleaning Like the Pros,* by Don Aslett (Dell, 1993). You, of course, *are* a pro, but this book still has loads of info worth checking out.
- *Clean It Fast, Clean It Right: The Ultimate Guide to Making Absolutely Everything You Own Sparkle and Shine,* edited by Jeff Bredenberg (Rodale Press, 1998).
- *How to Clean and Care for Practically Anything,* by the editors of *Consumer Reports* (Consumers Union, 2002).

Safe Transport of Cleaning Products

Tightly cap every cleaning product after use, and be doubly careful when you're putting your products into your vehicle. Keep all containers upright; you may want to experiment by inserting cardboard, bubble wrap, or other packing materials into your caddies to make sure the containers won't jostle around while you drive. Keep your products in the trunk; if you have an SUV or otherwise have to keep your materials with you in the vehicle itself, be sure it's always well ventilated.

Scheduling

You'll want to find a balance between a schedule that meets your own needs and one that meets your clients' needs. You might need to be more flexible as you start out; once you're in demand, you'll likely have a waiting list, and that gives you more control over your time. You will have a scheduling disaster at some point in your business: An unexpected crisis—small or large—can ruin the best-laid plans, bad weather could throw a wrench into things, or you might simply be overly optimistic about your timetable. There's nothing to do but muddle through as best you can—trusting that your clients will understand, perhaps offering reduced rates or makeup visits—and learn from the experience. Here are some other things to think about as you start to set up a housekeeping schedule:

■ How many houses can you reasonably clean in a day? Some cleaners cheerfully take on three or four jobs a day; others are worn out after a single home. Don't try to do more than you can complete and feel good about.

■ Take transportation time into account. How far is it between the homes you clean? Leave adequate time to get from one house to another, and don't forget the possibility of traffic jams, accidents, bad weather, car problems, and other causes for delay. You may also need time to stop at a gas station, convenience store, or bank between jobs.

■ How much extra time do you want to allow yourself in the schedule? If you leave yourself an hour to get from house to house when it generally takes only forty minutes, you'll feel more relaxed and in control. On the other hand, you may wish to maximize your number of jobs by having a tighter schedule.

■ Remember to allow time for meals, snacks, and breaks. Some cleaners are happy to eat in the car between jobs; others prefer to wait until they're done for the day; and still others like a set lunch break, allowing them a chance to unwind for a while. Think about how you'll be happiest, and schedule this time into each workday.

■ We all have errands and appointments that we need to take care of from time to time. You might need to see your doctor, accountant, lawyer, or printer during business hours. It's wise to have an open hour or two during each week for such events.

■ Don't forget to allow time for administrative work: record keeping, filing, answering e-mail, returning phone calls, and so on.

■ Having a partner—or even friendly helpers you can call on from time to time—makes logistics much simpler. Even if you prefer to service every client personally, aides can keep a schedule flowing smoothly when you'd be lost trying to do everything on your own. Think errands; running out of supplies; vacuum breakdown; staying late or arriving early to finish a particularly thorny or time-critical assignment.

- Breakdowns in scheduling happen to all of us, no matter how long we've been in business. Have a plan for dealing with these, and set it down in writing in your service manual. It's also wise to have client contact information close at hand wherever you go. If a scheduling problem comes up during the day, you'll know how to reach your clients to let them know.

The Victorian Housemaid

In Victorian times, if there was a dirty job to do, the housemaid was the one to do it. The housemaid was responsible for most of the dirty and backbreaking tasks that kept the household running. She was usually under the direct supervision of the housekeeper. In the early morning she swept the whole of the downstairs rooms; cleaned and raked out the grates in the fireplaces, removing the dead ashes and kindling from the night before; polished the grates; then laid a new fire in preparation for the day ahead. She also carried numerous heavy buckets of water upstairs, not only so that the household members could bathe, but also to do her daily chores with. Then she changed the bed linens, got rid of any fleas, lice, bedbugs, or other unwelcome guests, and then made the beds again. The upstairs received a thorough scrubbing. The housemaid also mended any household linen in need of repair.

Taking Care of Yourself

Having a solid support system is critical if you're starting a business. We've said it before, but it's worth repeating: You'll be working harder for yourself than you ever worked for anyone else. And you'll want—you'll need—people out there who can help you cope with all the new demands you'll be facing.

If you're lacking in the support department, think about ways you might fill in the gaps. Are there friends from the past you can reconnect with? Family members who've been there for you before? Support groups you can join or create? Even cleaning newsgroups and forums on the Internet can remind you that you're not alone. (Just be careful on the Net: You can't trust everyone or everything there.) Or perhaps a church, synagogue, or other spiritual group can provide you with connections and encouragement.

Don't forget to take time for yourself. What makes you feel special: a gourmet meal, a day off, a hot bath, a walk in the woods? Give it to yourself. Are you an animal lover? Visit your local humane society and spend an hour hugging the dogs and cats; you'll all benefit. (You may even be able to volunteer as an official cuddler.) And you can always try bartering your housecleaning services for those of a massage therapist! Here are some other tips that might help you feel good through a long and successful housecleaning career:

- **Take care of your feet.** You will be on your feet for a large part of every day, so it's worth investing in shoes that are comfortable and offer your feet the support they need. The type of shoe is up to you: athletic shoes, walking shoes, work shoes, or even soft slippers. There are a lot of great choices out there, and you should get what works best and is most comfortable for you. Go to a good shoe store and talk to the folks there about their recommendations. Make sure to give them a realistic picture of the demands you place on your feet.
- **Wear comfortable clothes.** Forget the latest fashions; what you need is clothing you can move in, not to mention lift, stretch, bend, and sweat in.
- **Watch how you lift.** If nothing else, you'll be lifting a vacuum cleaner a lot on this job, and chances are you'll be lifting other weights, too. Learn how to lift things safely, with your lower body, not your back. If you've ever injured your back even slightly, you'll understand how important this is. Even a tiny sprain can put you out of commission for weeks.
- **Watch for reactions to the products you use.** You'll be exposed to cleaning products more than most people are, so watch out for any adverse reactions you might have to them. You can also try using hypoallergenic and scent-free products; many cleaners prefer these (and so do many clients). Also see chapter 7 for suggestions on finding natural and eco-friendly green products to avoid chemical exposure entirely.
- **Wear good-quality rubber gloves.** Also, because you're likely (even with gloves on) to be exposing your hands to repeated wet-dry-wet cycles, treat them regularly with moisturizers. These can be a silky, sweet-smelling treat for the soul as well.

- **Take time off.** That's tough to do as an entrepreneur. You do have to sacrifice a lot of free time when you're starting up a new business venture, but don't sacrifice all of it. You need some downtime to relax, to reinvigorate yourself, to spend time with loved ones, to remind yourself what you're in business *for*. Find a balance that works right for you. It might mean guaranteeing yourself one full day off a week. It might mean taking a week off twice a year. It might mean unplugging the phone in the evening. Whatever "time off" means to you, you need it just as much as you need your clients and your sponges.

- **Watch for signs of burnout.** Being crabby and irritable all the time, feeling out of control of your emotions or moods, experiencing sleep disorders (maybe you want to sleep all the time, or perhaps you find yourself lying awake all night), losing interest in your work (or your family or friends), receiving complaints about the job you're doing: All of these are warning signs that scream *Lighten up!* Listen to them. Your career is on the line. Burnout can leave you out of commission forever.

- **Eat right.** You've heard this one before, but it's true. Having the right nutrients to keep your body fueled can be critical to getting through your demanding day. Eating regular, healthy, nonsugary meals and snacks will make you feel better and work better. (Still, every now and then, "eating right" can include a hot fudge sundae when you really, really need it.)

- **Music can be a great tool for staying sane.** If you're alone while you clean, you might be able to bring along a headphone-equipped music player or radio and listen to music you enjoy—just be sure the volume is low enough that you can still hear those important noises: doorbells, children, pets, intruders(!), and so on. Or you might enjoy listening to books on tape. If this isn't possible while you're cleaning, make sure you have plenty to listen to in the car while you're driving from job to job. Some people find that music can make administrative and record-keeping work a pleasure rather than a chore.

- **Exercise.** Yes, cleaning houses is demanding physical work, but it doesn't really qualify as aerobic exercise, the kind that keeps your heart and lungs and muscles healthy. Try to work some aerobic exercise into your weekly routine. Even going for walks can make a huge difference. You might enjoy swimming or bicycling—exercises you can do without being on your feet.

Both are low-impact and easy on overworked joints. Do be realistic, though. If you're feeling fatigued, sleep is probably more important than exercise. Your doctor or health-care provider can help you find a balance that's right for you.

- **Speaking of sleep, make sure to do it!** Everyone's sleep needs differ. If you're not used to being active all day, you might find that your sleep needs increase when you begin a housecleaning career. Pay attention to your body; if you're not getting enough sleep, it will let you know.
- **Stress-reduction techniques might help you, too.** Breathing techniques, yoga, meditation, visualization—all these can help you stay healthy and happy. It might all sound very New Agey, but it doesn't have to be. Breathing exercises can be about finding a spiritual center, but they can also serve as a simple relaxation technique; it's up to you. Investigate your local bookstores, the Internet, and community resources for information on dealing with stress. You'll find a lot of good workshops, classes, seminars, books, and much more out there for you.

07

The Green Housecleaner

Going green is the hottest trend in the cleaning business these days—and a whole lot of other businesses to boot. If you're not already thinking green, it's time you start.

What Is Green?

The Green Cleaning Network defines green cleaning on its Web site (www .greencleaningnetwork.org) as "cleaning to protect health without harming the environment." In her book *Green Home, Clean Home,* Kimberly Delaney describes what she calls "the green cleaning mind-set." It's a new attitude toward cleaning and health that says *What if applying chemicals isn't cleaning our homes; what if it's actually* polluting *them?*

It's certainly polluting the planet. Cleaning products are filled with unpronounceable chemicals known to damage human organs, interfere with our ability to have children and defend ourselves against disease, cause brain damage, and contribute to cancer. Breathing their fumes hurts your lungs; spilling them on your skin can burn you; ingesting them can kill you.

Once these substances hit the environment, they injure and kill animals. Many stay in the water or soil for—well, forever, or nearly so.

They do destroy germs and dirt. These are effective substances. When you're exhausted and pressed for time, these cleansers are The Bomb—in more ways than one. Are you still sure you want to devote your career to distributing them across the globe?

More and more housecleaners, manufacturers, and just plain folks are changing their thinking and turning green—a little or a lot. New cleaning products that are safer for people, pets, and the planet are appearing all the time. Old cleaning products—like vinegar, baking soda, lemon juice, club soda, and cornstarch—are coming back in a big way.

Why Green?

As a professional housecleaner, you have even more reason to consider greening up: your own well-being. If you use harsh chemicals throughout your workday, you're exposing yourself to their harsh side effects continually. The more time you spend breathing stinky fumes and immersing your hands in irritating fluids, the more damage you do to your health. Some cleaners find that their lungs, hands, or heads ache at the end of a day. Go green and you'll likely feel better immediately—not to mention the fact that you will avoid the long-term effects of bathing yourself in chemical soup dozens of hours a week.

There's another factor to consider, too. Green makes good business sense. You can attract more clients, charge higher fees, and make more money as a green cleaner. For real.

These are just some of the ways going green can benefit you and your company directly:

- Being an earth-friendly company positions you as a niche business, allows you to compete with bigger firms, and brings in potential customers who might have otherwise passed you by. Indeed, many green cleaners report that new clients seek *them* out, not the other way around!
- In fact, going green gives you *many* new selling points for your business, because the benefits not only extend to you and your clients, but also to your clients' kids, pets, the neighborhood, and the planet, well into the future. That's a lot of happiness you're adding to the world.
- Knowing how to clean—really clean—in ways that don't harm human or ecological health is a rare commodity. If you have this expertise, you can charge for it. Clients value this wisdom enough to pay more for it.
- It's the right thing to do. Nobody's in favor of polluting! And those house-cleaners who've gone green find a whole new level of satisfaction in their work. They're not just making money—they're making the world a better place. If the prospect of scrubbing one more toilet just does not leave you eager to leap into a new workday—well, saving the life of a wild salmon or preventing a case of childhood cancer just might.

Getting Started

Going green doesn't have to be either-or. You can dip a toe in the water and see what you think. Try a single green product and check out the results. Or go green for a single client who's willing to experiment with you. Chances are, some of your clients will be the ones suggesting the trial! A single greener moment in your cleaning day will indeed make a difference—perhaps in your health, certainly in the environment.

There are myriad products out there with different formulas, different scents, different strengths and weaknesses. Try a number of them and see which work best for you.

Unfortunately, you can't expect the same results. This is one of the difficult parts about going green: Natural substances that are easy on the world often do require harder work. Many are more expensive than their chemical counterparts as well. The trade-off is better health, but the choice is yours.

What's in Your Cleaning Bucket?

Take a look at the ingredients list of the products you clean with. (They may be listed on the label; if they're not, see below.) Here's what *not* to clean with:

- Sodium lauryl sulfate and sodium laureth sulfate (abbreviated as SLS or SLFS)
- Butyl cellosolve
- Diethanolamine (DEA)
- Triethanolamine (TEA)
- Alkylphenol ethoxylate (APE)
- Triclosan
- Phosphate
- Sodium hydroxide
- Artificial fragrance

All of these ingredients are toxic. Some cause cancer, others rashes, brain damage, or birth defects. Some contribute to species extinction. Take these products off your shopping list and the earth will breathe a little easier.

Another thing to watch out for is excessive packaging. A scary proportion of the garbage sent to landfills is packaging materials—often packaging that doesn't need to be there at all, or materials (like plastics and vinyls) made of petroleum and very,

very slow to break down. Petroleum products, of course, need oil—which is limited and growing more precious every day. Think of it this way: Do you want that barrel of oil to fuel an ambulance or heat a hospital—or do you want it turned into those plastic coatings over cleaning supplies that take half an hour even to open? Yeah, we thought so. (We call that packaging "consumer-proof.")

Green manufacturers often sell their products in refillable containers. That way you buy a container (often a really great-looking one) once, not daily or weekly. You then buy refills in bulk. It's a good system.

Any packaging that's made with "post-consumer waste" or "recycled materials," or that's labeled "biodegradable," earns more brownie points, too.

The Household Products Database

The Household Products Database (http://householdproducts.nlm.nih.gov) is maintained by the National Institutes of Health. This extensive online list allows you to look up specific products by brand name to get an idea of their ingredients and potential hazards. It's worth checking out each of the cleaning products you use here. It doesn't offer exhaustive information—the data is all taken from the Material Safety Data Sheets provided on each product by its manufacturer. Still, this is a great starting point for educating yourself and your clients. Some products may surprise you with their ingredients and known risks.

Green Tools

You can go green not just in your selection of cleaning products but also in the tools you use—from dusters and towels to vacuums and sponges. In fact, this is one of the most delightful ways to try greening up, because green cleaning tools are just plain cool. The machines are sleek, the fabrics are cuddly-soft, and the results can be awesome.

Because natural cleaning products may require more time and elbow grease to be effective, your cleaning toolkit is even more essential. You'll want top-quality brushes, sponges, scrubbies, mops, brooms, vacuums, and cleaning cloths to ease the tasks.

Your green toolkit might hold:

- **Buckets.** Stainless steel is more eco-friendly; plastic is lighter in weight and quieter.

- **Dry mop.** There's a bit of debate over how eco-friendly those Swiffer dry mops really are, but most cleaners find them easy and efficient. You can also attach cleaning cloths to a dry mop before use, then take them off, launder, and reuse.
- **Wet mop.** Sponge or string—it's your call! But again, you can attach a reusable cleaning cloth to make the mop last longer.
- **Microfiber cloths.** While this synthetic fabric does rely on petroleum, it's so efficient that it may be worth considering. Its millions of tiny fibers trap dirt and dust, and the fabric is washable and long-lasting.
- If microfiber isn't for you, **reusable cloths** can be made from recycled cotton jersey or flannel. Cut old shirts, pajamas, and T-shirts into washcloth-size pieces; if you have a sewing machine, a quick zigzag stitch around the edges can prevent fraying. Bring a stack with you to each cleaning job and then just throw them in the wash at the end of the day. They can last a year or more.
- **Sponges.** Twistclean.com sells truly spiffy sponges, or you can look for natural cellulose. Reuse sponges by microwaving or boiling after each use.
- **Brushes.** Look for natural bristles.
- **Squeegees** for glass, tubs, and appliances.

Is There a Green Vacuum?

Well, no. Not fully. Vacuums all use electricity; they all require energy and resources in manufacture (no one has yet perfected the all-palm-frond vacuum); they all require packaging and transportation to get to you. Still, there are better, more efficient, less wasteful vacuums.

Perhaps the best advice is simply to look for a vacuum that will last a long time. If you need a new appliance every few years, you'll be using up a lot of resources. Begin with a good-quality machine that lasts a few decades; the planet will thank you.

Look at both airflow and amps as well. A vacuum's airflow is measured in cubic feet per minute (cfm). The higher the airflow figure, the more suction power, the better the vacuum. Amps, on the other hand, simply measure how much electricity a vacuum uses. More amps doesn't necessarily mean a better vacuum. It just tells you that the vac uses more energy.

For green cleaners, a vacuum that features a HEPA (high-efficiency particulate

The Green Clean Institute

As yet, there are no universal standards for what constitutes "green." If a cleaner wants to call herself green or eco-friendly, she can; it's up to clients to find out what (if anything) that label really means.

The Green Clean Institute was founded to provide credentials for cleaners—to put some meaning and teeth behind that "green" claim. The company certifies individuals as Green Clean Technicians, Managers, and Executives; it also certifies entire companies.

The process isn't free, or easy. GCI requires that you complete downloadable courses for each credential, and pass a written test. Along with the certification, these courses also provide a thorough education in green cleaning—the kind of expertise it might take you years of on-the-job self-education to gain. And there's an online Green Janitor Directory that lists certified cleaners by area. For many cleaners, it's a good way to learn their new business and gain new clients. The price of the courses is tax-deductible.

Green Clean Institute, Inc.
2227 White Eagle Drive, Suite 201
Plainfield, IL 60586
(815) 609-4546 or (815) 272-1653
www.greencleaninstitute.com
office@greencleaninstitute.com
The Green Janitor Directory: www.greenjanitor.com

GreenSweep Natural Home Cleaners
(773) 697-8190
www.GreenSweepChicago.com
GreenSweep Natural Home Cleaners had its start when Michael and Jessica, two business majors, graduated from college and wanted to put their degrees to work by founding a company of their own. Problem was, as recent grads they had very few resources. And the economy wasn't looking very promising. Established firms were going belly-up. Consumers were finding themselves cutting *back* on spending.

"We wanted a company we could start up and operate ourselves," says Michael. "We had a lot of ideas for businesses, but when we thought about them, they were things we couldn't afford to start—we just didn't have the money.

"The idea of a cleaning business just came to us one day. We knew it didn't require a lot of capital." GreenSweep Natural Home Cleaners was born in early 2008.

The firm is located in the center of Chicago and services the metro area. It has both residential and commercial branches, and it specializes in environmentally friendly methods and products.

It was a good choice. "This is one of the best businesses out there," says Michael, "if you're willing to work hard. We both wanted freedom and control over our destiny. We had energy to give. This is a great business if you find yourself in that position."

Even as the economy grew worse, GreenSweep took off. Within eight months, the company had thirty to thirty-five clients signed up for routine service: some weekly, some biweekly, some monthly. "And we hope to expand," Michael says. "In fact, we're looking for employees right now."

He credits the green mission with much of that overwhelming success. "Green is good," he says, "for two reasons. First, as a business model it's very popular right now, and it's going to continue to grow in the near future. Second, as a green company we're a niche business. People seek *us* out. If customers do an Internet search for, say, residential cleaners, they get Merry Maids, Molly Maids, big corporations. We tend to get lost. As a specialized firm, though, we are able to compete. People searching for green cleaners will find us right away."

Both founders enjoy the work. "On a personal level," Michael says, "it's allowed me to control my own destiny—my own schedule—my own lifestyle. I don't have to wait for a paycheck. I can make money every day, even every night, as long as I'm willing to do the work." That's a powerful motivator.

Cleaning in harmony with the environment is also satisfying. "I live this lifestyle anyway," Michael says. "And if you're smart about the products, if you really know their benefits, you can really use that to meet your clients' needs. You can also get some great cost savings that way." GreenSweep uses 100 percent green products. Most come from Shaklee, and the firm has been happy with the results. "We sometimes use others for certain applications," he adds.

The work is hard, he admits. "You have to clean all day, then go home and work on the administrative functions as well. And you have no choice but to stay at the computer until it's done. It can also be challenging to schedule the appointments. Sometimes just the logistics of getting to each job—especially in downtown Chicago—can be overwhelming."

Still, for those ready to make the commitment, it's a great opportunity. "It helps to have a partner," Michael says in conclusion. "And I recommend that in any business—but especially this one—you try to figure out not just your strengths but also what you do *not* know. Then find out how to get the answers you need. The resources are out there, and there are people who can get you the information you need. Take the time to seek them out."

air) filter is an important, if not crucial investment. These models remove almost all particles (think dust, pollens, allergens) from the air. They cost more, but they create better air quality, healthier homes, and healthier clients. Your customers may demand a HEPA filter—and it makes a fine selling point for your business.

Some vacuums use bags that need frequent changing, which can be wasteful. Bagless vacuums, on the other hand, may need to have their filters changed often— which can also be wasteful. A bagless vac with a washable filter may be a good bet. Then again—as always in cleaning—your *best* bet is what works for you.

Green Cleaning Resources

Books

Most of the green housecleaning books available now are aimed at individuals looking to improve their own lives and housekeeping, with recipes for herbal and other natural cleaners. Still, they offer lots of ideas, tips, inspiration, and advice on what to look for (and avoid) in green products. The following are worth checking out:

Better Basics for the Home: Simple Solutions for Less Toxic Living by Annie Berthold Bond (Three Rivers Press, 1999)

Clean and Green: The Complete Guide to Non-Toxic and Environmentally Safe Housekeeping by Annie Berthold-Bond (Ceres Press, 1994)

Clean Home, Green Home: The Complete Illustrated Guide to Eco-Friendly Homekeeping by Kimberly Delaney (Globe Pequot Press, 2009)

Clean House, Clean Planet by Karen Logan (Pocket Books, 1997)

Green Clean: The Environmentally Sound Guide to Cleaning Your Home by Linda Mason Hunter and Mikki Halpin (Melcher Media, 2005)

Green Cleaning: Everything You Need to Know About Providing Environmentally Friendly Cleaning Services is an 80-page downloadable e-book available from www.thejanitorialstore.com. The Web site itself may be worth a look for its collection of resources and support for cleaning professionals. Much of its content is available only to members (a fee is charged), but *Green Cleaning* can be downloaded by nonmembers as well.

Green This! Volume 1: Greening Your Cleaning by Deirdre Imus (Simon & Schuster, 2007)

Web Sites

- www.greenerchoices.org (from *Consumer Reports*). Much like *National Geographic,* this objective, long-established magazine offers unimpeachably reliable information.
- http://greenercleaner.blogspot.com
- www.lime.com
- www.naturalhomemagazine.com
- www.thegreenguide.com (from *National Geographic*). This great Web site includes Buying Guides listing the best value and greenest product in many categories (if only it were larger!).

Manufacturers

New companies are (yay!) going green all the time. The following is a woefully inadequate list of some reputable manufacturers whose products may be worth a try. Their Web sites have helpful greening-up advice as well. If you start with these firms, by all means don't stop with them!

- Begley's Best (www.begleysbest.com)
- Bi-O-Kleen (http://biokleenhome.com)
- Dr. Bronner (www.drbronner.com)
- Earth Friendly Products (www.ecos.com)
- Ecover (www.ecover.com)
- Howard Naturals (www.howardnaturals.com)
- Method (www.methodhome.com)
- Mrs. Meyer's (www.mrsmeyers.com)
- Seaside Naturals (www.seasidenaturals.com)
- Seventh Generation (www.seventhgeneration.com)
- Shaklee (www.shaklee.com)
- Twist (www.twistclean.com). Twist sells eco-friendly scrubbies, sponges, and cleaning cloths of all kinds with flair.

08 Understanding and Serving Customers

The housecleaning field requires a sense of dedication and a true commitment to customer service. Because you will be relying heavily on word of mouth to advertise your business, excellent customer service is mandatory. Without it, your business may never get off the ground.

The key to customer service is to remember that all of us are customers ourselves. Think about some of the businesses and services that you frequent, and why. You might choose to do business at a bank that has slightly higher fees than others nearby, for instance, because of the way you're treated: You're always greeted with a smile, and the banking representatives, who know you by name, ask how business is going and how the weather's treating you. Such interactions can make you feel like not simply a customer but a valued friend.

The more you know about your clients, the better you'll be able to service them. Just remembering names and addresses isn't enough in this day and age. You should always know your clients' cleaning needs, of course, but remembering some personal information will serve you well, too. Putting that extra touch into your business dealings will go a long way toward keeping your clients happy, and it will help you cultivate new clients as well. Making clients feel special helps establish trust, a vital ingredient in any entrepreneurial endeavor. It's especially crucial in housecleaning, too, because customers are inviting you into their personal, private space.

Excellent service also establishes your credibility. Clients will be much more comfortable knowing that you don't think of them just as a job to be done. Moreover, a client who's happy and feels that you care will lead you to other potential clients. Your ability to provide excellent customer service can be the key to building your business into a successful and prosperous one.

(Some sample client information records are included in chapter 10.) First impressions are usually long-lasting ones. From your initial consultation on, the better you present yourself, the better your company will look to prospective customers. Pay attention to details: Notice the sort of decorations and artwork in a client's home, for example. If you make the client feel that her or his home is special, the client will have a better feeling about you coming in to clean it.

Melinda's Story

I keep a card file with client information: birth dates, pets' names, children's names, known medical issues, job title, and any special holidays they observe. This gives me the opportunity to personally congratulate clients on job promotions; wish them a happy birthday, a pleasant Rosh Hashanah, or a happy Easter; and inquire about their health. I have several clients with seasonal allergies, and I often inquire as to whether or not the pollen is more severe this year than last. Little things like these all go a long way toward making people feel they're more than just paying clients.

Five Essential Elements of Customer Service

1. Be courteous and friendly.

This should be a given, but many people can go an entire day without doing it. Being courteous and friendly costs you nothing and will go a long way toward making customers happy—not only with you, but also with the service you have provided. A friendly and courteous manner helps establish trust and generates understanding between you and your customers.

2. Stay focused on your customers.

When you are with customers, always maintain eye contact. Not only does this imply honesty, but it also shows respect. Don't do other things—turning your back, washing your hands—while engaged in a conversation with a client. Yes, you're there to provide a service, but you're also there to pay attention to the client. Treat each client as if she or he is your only one.

3. Ask questions.

You won't be able to offer outstanding customer service unless you're able to determine what the customer expects. You can help your customers outline their specific needs by asking specific questions of them. Talk to them about their needs and preferences. Give them different options and help them find what will work best for them. Does the client prefer that you leave the toilet seats down, or that you not open the windows while working? Think about how you'd like to perform the assignment, and get feedback from the client.

4. Listen to your customers.

Now that you have asked the questions, you need to listen to the answers given to you. Pay close attention to the client's responses, write them down as soon as you have a moment, and use this information to help your customers get what they want. Offer your advice and expertise, but don't talk over the client. You have to put your active listening skills to work! If you don't understand something, ask for clarification. This way you'll both have a clear understanding of the services that will be provided.

5. Follow through on your service.

No matter how courteous and friendly you are, no matter how focused you may be, regardless of how many questions you might have asked, and no matter how long and hard you have listened, none of this will matter if you don't follow through with your client. If you say that you'll have the house plan completed by Friday, be sure that it's completed and delivered to the client on Friday. Keeping your promises is

The Victorian Lady's Maid

The duties of the lady's maid were to assist the lady of the household with her clothing, her hair, and her toilet. The lady's maid spent the majority of her time in choosing the lady's wardrobe, keeping it in good condition, cleaning stains from the delicate fabric, and refurbishing it when fashions dictated. She sometimes created lotions and makeup for her lady. As an incentive to do her job well, most of the lady's maids were given cast-off clothing and would usually receive all the lady's clothing when the lady died.

the most important aspect of excellent customer service, and yet the most over-looked. If you offered a special service, be sure the customer receives it. Not to do so is the surest and quickest way to become unemployed!

These five elements are not all that's encompassed by the term *customer service*, but they are indeed essential. Without these five ingredients, your service will fall flat. Recite the five essential guidelines as a mantra. When the going gets tough, and a client is being uncooperative, recite your mantra. Do what it takes (within reason, of course) to keep a client happy. A happy customer will usually spread the word to others seeking the same dependable, reliable, and exceptional service that you have provided. All it takes is some dedication on your part and a commitment to treating others the way you would expect to be treated. Take the time to know your customers. Laugh with them and enjoy their company. Be genuine and show that your company cares about them, not just as customers but as individuals as well. And remember to smile!

Linda S.

Minneapolis

Linda S. may be one of the best housecleaners in Minneapolis. She's certainly one of the humblest. "I don't really consider this a career," she says. "It's just what I do. I'm always afraid I can't do this well enough, or that I don't deserve to charge so much."

Her clients would wholeheartedly disagree. Listen to Linda describe her work and you'll get a sense of what makes her special.

"You have to be conscientious. Sometimes you have to clean things that don't really look dirty. You might think, *Well, I don't see any dirt*—but other people do. You have to open your eyes to what might need cleaning. I have a kind of guilt complex: If I don't clean it, someone else might look at it and notice that I didn't. I'll get down on my hands and knees to dust under the furniture. I'll pick things up to dust them and dust underneath them. I like to do little extra touches—things like cleaning the soap dishes or cleaning the shower walls. It depends on the client, but I try to add something she'll remember and like.

"The bigger cleaning companies won't pick things up or go to any trouble. If there's a newspaper lying on the floor, they won't pick it up to vacuum underneath it. I'm more thorough; I like to give extra service. If I find a penny on the floor, I pick it up and put it on a table." Indeed, if Linda spots a *pin* on the floor, she picks it up and puts it in a bowl to make sure pets or children don't get at it.

She's never advertised; 100 percent of her business has come from word of mouth, and she's had so much that she prefers to leave her last name out of this book, lest she get even more calls!

"I started in about 2000, and I got my start from helping my sister Nancy. She'd been cleaning houses for a while at that point. There was a program in her area where, if people had disabilities, they'd pay to get them help with their cleaning. Nancy did a lot of cleaning through this program, and as time went by, more people discovered that she had cleaning experience. Soon she was busy enough that she needed some assistance.

"I was working in a bank at the time, and I like this job much better. You're mostly on your own. There, I'd get exhausted from smiling all day long, and you never really see that you've made a difference.

"Now every client that I have has been from that original group. It's all been word of mouth." The sisters still work together on occasion. "It works out well. It's nice to have someone there with you, even if you're cleaning in separate parts of the house; it's just nice to have the company! We laugh together. She's better at coping than I am. I hate mopping, and she doesn't mind it, so she does all the mopping.

"I like to clean," Linda continues. "When you're done, you're done, and you can see the results. Some things are hard, of course. You do have a lot of aches and pains. You have to watch out not to pick things up the wrong way. And there are no sick days or benefits. If you're sick, or the weather's bad, people still count on you to get there."

"I know my limits. I can clean for about five hours; then I'm physically beat. I've been able to schedule around that, though.

"I like being able to satisfy others. When a client is happy with how her house looks, I feel terrific. All the people we work for are great. A lot of them become friends. People trust me. I don't really know why, but they trust me, and that feels good. Sometimes we end up talking, and I always stop to chat with them—off the clock, of course!"

With this kind of work ethic and commitment to customer service, clients are fanatically loyal to Linda, sticking with her through their own divorces, deaths in the family, even moves to other parts of the city. "I don't raise my rates very often," she admits, "but most of my customers have given *me* raises. I have some very nice people that I clean for!"

After years as a housecleaner, Linda's gradually starting to think about slowing down. She has a word of advice for those just starting out and hoping for the kind of success she's seen: "Start slowly and hang in there. Don't count on this being your sole existence until you get a good roster of clients. It does take a while. Be patient, if you can. Start little by little.

"And when you get a job, do more than everyone else would." It's certainly worked for Linda. It can work for you, too.

Housecleaners and Pets

Companion animals are more and more frequent presences in our homes, and for good reason. If you instinctively love animals, dealing with clients' companions can indeed be one of the most rewarding parts of your job.

It's not required, however. Of primary concern is your own safety. If there's any chance that a pet could become vicious or even unpredictable, discuss the situation thoroughly with your client. Don't hesitate to turn down a job or to withdraw your services if there's an animal around that makes you uncomfortable.

Furthermore, even the kindest and gentlest of pets can be forever underfoot. This can add time, energy, and complications to your day. If you'd rather not do your work around pets, for any reason, feel free to insist that all animals be crated or otherwise confined during your cleaning visits. This is an entirely reasonable request.

All that being said, "pet-friendly" does make a great selling point for cleaners these days. If you can make friends with a client's pets—especially timid or sensitive pets—you may have a client who will bond to you for life.

The first step is to talk to your clients about their companions. Some clients may prefer that you not interact with their pets—the animals could be following demanding training regimens, for example, or they might have special dietary or medical needs that limit your involvement. Be sure to abide by whatever pet guidelines are set.

In most cases, however, clients are happy to find cleaners who appreciate and enjoy their animals. Find out what each companion is like, and whether the client has any advice about approaching, feeding, playing with, or otherwise being involved with the four-legged members of the family. Remember that the cleaning process is generally noisy and chaotic, which can be scary for a lot of animals—which are, after all, having their own private territories invaded with no say in the matter. Be sensitive to this, and never force your company on a nervous animal. It may be that Fluffy's only desire in your presence is to hide in the farthest corner of the closet and not move a whisker until you leave—and that's Fluffy's call to make. Respect it.

Still, many animals will relax around you, either sooner or later. With your client's approval, you might want to encourage the process by offering food treats, toys, or simple attention. Go ahead and talk to the animals. Stroke them if they enjoy it. Toss them a toy (carefully!). Attach a ball or feather to your vacuum for them to chase. Some cautions are in order, though:

- Cleaning products can be toxic to pets, even in small doses (smaller than would cause harm to a human). Use extra care with your products if animals are present. Never leave an open jar or bottle unattended—put the cap back on firmly if you'll be turning away from it, even for an instant. Know whether your products might give off fumes harmful to pets, and be prepared to offer safer alternatives. Know what to do if a pet does inadvertently ingest any of your products. Natural cleaning products are healthier for pets (not to mention people and planets), but they do still offer risks. Don't let down your guard just because your products are green.

- Take extra care as you move and clean around the house. Pets may be hiding in or around any corner, and you don't want to startle them, or, worse, accidentally step on, bump, or run into them.
- Animals are extremely sensitive to odors, and you may be bringing the scents of other critters with you when you arrive at a cleaning job—perhaps from your own pets, or other clients', or from animals you run into in your daily life. Be aware that this can frighten pets or lead to unpredictable behavior. A lot of what seems to be mystifying pet behavior—"Her mood just snapped out of the blue!"—may actually be a response to new or threatening odors.
- Always keep toilet lids down. Even if your clients themselves don't seem to pay attention to this, be sure those lids are shut on your watch.
- Know your clients' policies on whether the pets are allowed outdoors or not, and follow them. If the animals should not be allowed out, be prepared to take extra care every time you open a door or even a window. Pets are often eager to go out whether it's permissible or not, and they can be quite crafty about getting their way. (We know of one cat who slithered out a dryer vent, a second-story bedroom window, *and* a broken screen door.) You don't want to be responsible for the heartache of a lost pet.
- Have your client leave contact information for veterinarians prominently in the house—perhaps on the fridge door or next to the phone. Discuss what to do if an emergency arises.

Finally, you may wish to do some extra research on the cleaning challenges associated with pets. Animals love us so much, they often leave little "surprises" all over the house; you'll want to know what to do with them. Sometimes these are left in the middle of the floor, but you may also find them in the darkest corners that only housecleaners seem to enter. Take a trip to your local pet store to explore the myriad products now available for dealing with pet hair, urine, odors, and fleas. For more specifics, see "Stuff that Stains" on page 84, or check out *Pet Clean-Up Made Easy,* by Don A. Aslett (Avon, MA: Adams Media, 2005).

Treated with respect, kindness, and sensitivity, your clients' companion animals can sweeten your professional life immeasurably. Enjoy!

Setting Up the Home Office

The housecleaning business doesn't happen just in houses. Billing, marketing, licensing, scheduling, and myriad other administrative tasks need a home, too. Cleaners' offices can be found in basements, attics, spare rooms, dining rooms, and even walk-in closets. An extra bedroom or den area is ideal, but with some ingenuity you can create a workable space in the corner of a room that is currently being used. You might even convert a pantry into your home office. Wherever you set up, though, there are some things you'll need.

Basic Equipment

All well-stocked housecleaners should have the following items—eventually. You might not be able to afford all of them right away, and that's okay. A computer, in particular, can be both expensive and intimidating. It will be worth the time and energy you put into acquiring and learning to use it—we can guarantee that. But don't feel that you can't begin cleaning clients' homes until you have a computer (or the other equipment listed here). It will be more complicated, but it can be done.

Separate Phone Line with Voice Mail

Having a dedicated business line is a must! An extra phone line costs about $25 a month. When clients are telephoning, you don't want your personal answering machine to pick up the call, nor do you want small children answering the phone. Solve problems before they start by getting a separate telephone line with voice mail; either buy an answering machine or have voice mail added to your regular telephone service. Also, be sure the telephone jack is located near your desk space. You don't want to have to get up out of your chair and walk to another room to answer your business line. (A portable phone would work, too.) Leave your voice mail on whenever you aren't at your desk.

A cell phone is another great option that gives you even more flexibility. Be sure the area where you live and clean gets strong reception before you invest.

Large Table or Computer Armoire

You needn't invest in a big, expensive desk. People are always attracted to large desks with lots of drawers. The drawers, however, encourage clutter and take up too much valuable space for a small area. A table is a much better choice. You might find something at a secondhand store; if the surface is in poor condition, paint over it with a high-gloss paint or simply cover it with an attractive tablecloth. The table must be sturdy enough to hold a computer and a few accessories, and tall enough to fit some metal file cabinets beneath. Be sure that the table you purchase is lightweight, so that you'll be able to move it if you need to. The desk area should be large enough to accommodate your entire setup: phone, computer components, printer, and scanner.

We wouldn't spend more than $100 for a table. If you can't find anything for less than $100, try a home-improvement store that has a lumber department. You can purchase a huge unfinished wooden tabletop nearly 4 inches thick for about $40. You can stain or paint it, and support the corners atop four metal storage cabinets. Throw a tablecloth over it, and no one will ever know the difference.

Armoires are terrific pieces of office furniture—like an office on wheels! Armoires are simply tall cabinets, much like a wardrobe or standing cabinet. The inside is carefully fitted with compartments to house your computer setup. Some even have a pullout table for writing, thus eliminating the need for a desk or table. The downside is that they can be expensive, starting at around $400 and ranging up to a few thousand dollars. Sometimes you can find them in secondhand stores, as well as in the classifieds. The advantage of using an armoire is that once you close the door, you've closed the office.

Comfortable Chair

You'll be spending considerable time sitting and doing administrative work, so you need a comfortable chair. Comfort and cost go hand in hand, so avoid the bargain chairs. There's little worse than working at a computer for two hours while sitting in a chair that has no back or lumbar support. The next day your back will let you know that it's not pleased with you!

You can sometimes find great deals on chairs at thrift stores or used–office-furniture stores. Be sure to get lumbar support, and think about choosing a chair that rolls easily on the surface of your floor. The less expensive chairs don't roll easily. If you have carpeting in your home office, you'll need a special hard plastic mat under the rolling chair. This prevents your carpet from being damaged. Similarly, if you have hardwood floors, a rubber mat will protect the floor and prevent the chair from rolling out of control.

Be sure to select a model that can be adjusted easily, both in height and in back position; a simple lever is ideal. With some of the less expensive chairs, you need a screwdriver to adjust the height—not very convenient. The chair's back should adjust to allow you to sit back or straight up. A good chair will cost about $125 brand new. The investment is worth it!

File Cabinets

One or two locking file cabinets should be sufficient. Lightweight metal cabinets are easy to clean, and they can be emptied and moved with little effort. It's important to keep paper file copies as backups to your digital copies. If your computer ever goes on the blink, you'll be able to refer to the paper copies. You are dealing with confidential information (for instance, you probably have the codes to your clients' home burglar alarms), so it's best to lock the paper copies and the CD-ROMs inside the file cabinets. If anyone enters your office, she or he won't be able to open the cabinet and go through the files. The tricky part is finding a safe place to store file cabinet keys. It's a good idea to have two sets, hidden in two separate places. Don't hide keys in a desk drawer, under a desk plant, or under the keyboard. Those are the first places a would-be burglar will look!

Fireproof Safe

A safe is a must because you'll be storing client's house keys, and clients need to know that these keys are secure. For even more security, be sure that your safe is fireproof. Although nothing is 100 percent fireproof, most models will withstand temperatures of 1,850 degrees Fahrenheit for two hours.

You can purchase a good-quality small fireproof safe with a combination or key lock for around $120. We don't recommend the electronic touch-pad models; they're expensive, starting at around $250, and if something goes wrong with the keyboard, you can't access the safe. If you have a combination or key lock safe and something happens to the locks, you can always call a locksmith.

Never get into the habit of leaving clients' keys on your table or desk or in your car. Keep the keys locked in the safe at all times when not in use. Make a habit of going to the safe the minute you walk in the door.

A medium-size safe works best. Small safes can easily be picked up and carried away should your home ever be burglarized. Safes can be covered with a tablecloth and used as a table; no one need ever know what's beneath it. You could also put the safe in the back of a closet. Keep it out of sight of windows and doors. People should be able to sit in or walk around your office and never see the safe. Wall models are terrific: The safe is set into the wall and covered by a picture. Given the price tag of the safe itself and of installation, however, wall safes are not cost-effective for most people.

The Victorian Scullery Maid

A scullery maid's day was spent mostly in the kitchen. Working under the supervision and direction of the cook, her duties fell to washing all dishes, pots, and pans. She also blackened and lighted the stoves in the mornings and cleaned the scullery, larders, kitchen, and servants' quarters. She was responsible for keeping the entire kitchen area clean and free from any rodents that might be present in the larder.

Combination locks can be difficult if you're in a hurry. The more hurried you are, the more often you'll stop at the wrong number or turn the dial in the wrong direction, resulting in frustration. Key locks are easiest, provided that you've hidden the key in an easy-to-remember place. Never store the keys to the safe with clients' house keys or your personal keys. It's just too easy to lose them.

Computer

The biggest purchase that you'll make—if you don't own one already—is a home computer. If you're in the market for a computer, don't be dazzled by all the bells and whistles. For your business, a basic model will do just as well as the higher-priced ones. Monitor size is a matter of personal preference; some people like larger monitors, but a smaller model can be a great space saver. Expect to spend anywhere from $700 to $1,500 for a basic computer. There are also more and more bare-bones computers available these days, for prices starting at less than $300. Expect this trend to continue.

It's best to stick with a name brand; unfamiliar manufacturers come and go, while the familiar brands have customer service divisions to help you if you ever have a problem. Once you select a computer and set it up, you'll want to choose an Internet service provider (ISP). Chapter 13 will tell you all you need to know about using the Web in your business. You can generate a huge amount of business as a result of your Web presence. Whether you have your own Web site or not, you'll definitely want e-mail for client contacts.

Office Machines

In addition to your computer, you'll need equipment that allows you to:

- print (flyers, business cards, bills, Guide to Services, and so on)
- scan (transfer photos and documents to your computer, where you can use them in your promotional literature or on your Web site)
- copy
- fax

You can buy separate machines to fulfill all of these functions—and if you need advanced or professional-level quality in any of them, separate machines are probably the way to go. They exist in every conceivable price range, from forty bucks on up to many thousands.

For most housecleaners and most home offices, however, multifunction machines are a great choice, especially when you're just starting out. These days you can buy a single machine that prints, scans, copies, and faxes (or any combination thereof). An acceptable-quality all-in-one machine can be purchased for $100 to $200.

Here are some questions to consider as you sort through the many models available:

- How user-friendly is the machine?
- Is it compatible with my computer and operating system?
- Does it come with all the cables needed for connecting to my computer and/or telephone jack? (Most do, but you want to know this before you make your purchase.)

- What kind of ink cartridges does it need? How readily available are these in my area, and how much do they cost? The price of a one- or two-month supply of ink may in fact be greater than that of the machine itself, so this is a crucial factor.
- What is the manufacturer's track record for reliability and technical support?

A good office-supply salesclerk should be able to provide you with all the information you need. It's also a good idea to research your various options in *Consumer's Digest, Consumer Reports,* or similar product guides. Online, type "product ratings" into any search engine and you'll find myriad Web sites filled with consumer reviews and experiences.

Other Supplies to Keep on Hand

- 8½-by-11-inch paper puncher (allows you to keep your documents and service manuals in three-ring binders)
- stapler
- pens and pencils
- CD-ROMs and storage case
- dry erase board to use as a calendar
- copy paper
- paper-recycling bin
- index cards and storage box
- Rolodex

Privacy

Once you set up your workspace, make it clear to your household and family members that the space is absolutely off-limits to anyone except you. At no time should a spouse, friend, or child be in the office. The office is a place to conduct business and nothing else. Instruct household and family members that when you are in your office, you are not to be disturbed. This means children, friends, family, neighbors—everyone! This can be tough for household members who think of you as being home and not working from home. Try hanging a DO NOT DISTURB sign on the door.

Boundaries

Treat your home business as you would any other professional place of business. This means setting business hours for yourself. Give yourself a schedule—every day from 6:00 to 8:00 a.m., for example. Then stick to it. You should spend the time in your office dealing with administrative tasks, planning, marketing, reading business literature, and so forth. When the scheduled time is over, get up and leave the office space. Don't be tempted to make personal telephone calls or catch up on personal correspondence during business hours. Combining business with your personal affairs can be a trap. Likewise, don't use family time or personal time to take care of business. You may have to experiment with several types of work schedules until you find one that works for you.

10 Record Keeping

Like cleaning itself, record keeping is a bit of an individual affair; only you know exactly what procedures will work best for you. There are, however, some minimum records that you must keep for tax purposes. Know that the more detailed your records, the better off you'll be.

Expense reports allow you to analyze your spending in detail and discover how you can save money: Perhaps you're paying for advertising that doesn't work, or maybe your car maintenance bills are heftier than they ought to be.

Income records give you a clear picture of the money you have available to you at any moment, and the money you can expect to receive. They also help you keep track of late payments and discover patterns in clients' payment histories. All this information is vital if you want to have a complete picture of your business.

As a small start-up, record keeping should be fairly simple and straightforward. If you take out a loan at any point in the future, however, banks will need detailed business records. And if you decide to become an employer, detailed record keeping will be a legal necessity. For all these reasons, good record keeping is a habit well worth getting into from the very beginning.

Client records are important in this business as well. The more you know and remember about your clients—their needs, their interests, their quirks, their preferences—the better you can serve them. Clients are trusting you with their homes, their possessions, their keys. It's vital that you have contact information for clients, police, poison control, home-alarm-system providers, and the like at your fingertips at all times.

So where do you begin? This chapter contains some sample records for a housecleaning business; they may offer you a starting point. There are excellent software programs and manual accounting systems available at stationery or office-supply stores that will set you up with all the records you'll need.

Cash or Accrual?

The first decision you'll need to make as you begin keeping business records is whether to use the cash system or the accrual system. You must choose one or the other and use it consistently.

In the cash system, you record each payment that you receive when you receive it; you record each expense when you pay it. If you bill a client on January 1 and she doesn't pay you until January 18, you record the transaction in your accounts on January 18. If you buy supplies via credit card, taking home your purchases on January 10 but not actually paying your credit card bill until January 25, you record the expense as occurring on January 25.

The accrual system involves recording payments and expenses on the date the transaction occurred, rather than the date that the money was actually paid or received. If you use the accrual system and bill a client on January 1, you'd list the payment in your records as occurring on January 1. The supplies you took home on January 10 would be listed on January 10.

Of the two systems, cash is the simpler. You keep your records much the way you maintain your checkbook register. Unless you maintain a large inventory (unlikely as a housecleaner) or extend credit to your clients (ditto), we recommend the cash system. If you use an accountant or bookkeeper, however, it's worth finding out her or his opinion on the question. Your adviser knows your own situation best.

The Business Checkbook

Your business checkbook is your first line of record-keeping defense. Remember to use your account only for business purposes. Reconcile your account against your bank statement every month. Not only will you stay on top of your income and expenses, but you'll be able to catch any errors and correct them quickly.

Mileage Records

Chances are you'll be using your car to drive from cleaning job to cleaning job. If you do, you'll need to keep track of all your business mileage: every mile, every fraction of a mile. As you'll see in chapter 11, there are two different ways to record automobile expenses and deduct them from your taxable income, but both of them require you to have a mileage record. If you don't write it down, you can't claim it as a deduction. Miles quickly add up to dollars at tax time.

Your best bet is to keep a small notebook right in your car; the glove compartment is a good home for it. Make a habit of writing down the beginning mileage at the start of every business trip, no matter how short. When you reach your destination, write down the closing mileage. You can do the math right on the spot if you like, or save this task for later; the important thing is to get your mileage written down. If your car has a trip counter (a special odometer that can be reset at the start of each journey), by all means use it and save yourself some time!

Income Records

Your income is the payments received from clients. You can record this information on a simple chart (see sample below). For each payment, you should record the client's name, the invoice date, the date you received payment, and the payment type (if it's by check, record the check number as well). Also, save any and all documentation verifying your income: your bank statements, credit card documents, online payment records, and so on. Keep all these documents in their own spot: a file in your file cabinet, a basket on your desk, even a shoe box. The point is to have all your documents in one safe place.

Expense Records

Expenses are a little more complicated than income. First of all, you should know that there are three types of business expenses: direct, indirect, and capital. **Direct expenses** are what the IRS calls "ordinary and necessary" costs, the stuff you have to pay for simply to run a business. They include cleaning supplies, office supplies, transportation expenses, advertising, and so on. These are the expenses you'll want to keep close track of.

Again, you'll want to keep documentation (sales receipts, canceled checks, credit card statements) for all your direct expenses, and these documents should be stored in their own separate, safe place. You should also record each expense in an expense ledger, either on paper or on a computer spreadsheet. For a start-up cleaning business, it's probably adequate to do this recording once a month; if you expand, however, and especially if you hire employees, you might want to keep weekly records.

Indirect expenses are the costs of running your home office, based on the percentage of your home that you use. Chapter 11 has all the information you need

Inv. #	Date	Client	Amt.	Date Paid	Pmt. Type (including check #)	Comments

to calculate your indirect expenses. In brief, if 10 percent of your house (based on square footage) is used as your home office, you can then deduct 10 percent of your house expenses from your taxable income; these expenses would include rent or mortgage, insurance, heat, electricity, and so on. As a cleaning business, you can calculate these expenses once a year (or have your accountant or tax preparer do so) to include on your tax returns. You could keep records of these expenses every month—and of course, it's not a bad idea to do so!—but as a small service provider, this is probably overkill.

Capital expenses are incurred when you purchase expensive equipment that will serve your business for many years. As a cleaner, this would most likely include

	Jan	Feb	Mar	Apr	May	Year
Advertising						
display ads						
flyers						
other						
Auto						
gas						
tolls						
maintenance						
insurance						
other						
Insurance						
liability insurance						
bonding						
Professional services						
legal						
accounting						
other						
Office expenses						
Internet service						
telephone						
cell phone						
business cards						
office supplies						
merchant acc't fees						
checking acc't fees						
Cleaning supplies						
Cleaning equipment						
License fees						
Other expenses						
Total expenses						

your computer and vacuum cleaner. Rather than deducting the entire cost of such a purchase from your taxable income in the year you bought it, you'd want to deduct the cost of a year's worth of use, also known as *depreciation*. Your tax preparer can provide you with information about depreciation, or see IRS Publications 334 (*Tax Guide for Small Business*) and 946 (*How to Depreciate Property*). Both can be viewed or downloaded for free at www.irs.gov.

For your purposes, then, expense records should focus on direct expenses; you and/or your tax preparer will worry about indirect and capital expenses at tax time. Below is a sample of a monthly direct business expense record you might use. The more detailed you can be in categorizing your expenses, the more useful the information will be. You might want to break down the Telephone category, for instance, into basic service charges, long-distance fees, voice-mail system, and fax. If your telephone bill is of concern to you (maybe it's just too high, or maybe it suddenly shoots up one month), having such detailed records will help you analyze the problem and figure out how to solve it.

To keep up-to-date with your expense reports, sit down once a month and go through all of the invoices and other expense documentation that you've set aside in its special place. Categorize each payment, then add them up and insert them on this form. You've now got a simple at-a-glance picture of where your money goes. Add the monthly totals to get the yearly figure when preparing your tax return.

Monthly Net Income Statement

Once you have monthly income and expense records, you can compare the two in a simple income statement. For the purposes of a housecleaning business, a simple statement like the one shown here should give you a picture of your business's health.

Sample Record: Monthly Net Income Statement

total receipts	$_____
– total expenses	$_____
= net income	$_____
– estimated taxes	$_____
= actual income	$_____

Client Records

As we've noted in chapter 8, having client information available at your fingertips can be invaluable to your business. You'll be able to give top-notch customer service by reminding yourself of each client's preferences, special dates, and family members. And you'll always know how to reach the client and anyone else you need to contact if a problem arises. Following are some sample client records.

Client Name _____

Address _____

Home telephone _____

Work telephone _____

Cell phone _____

E-mail address _____

Pets _____

Home alarm system _____ yes _____ no

Home alarm system code and instructions _____

_____

_____

_____

Contact information for home alarm system provider _____

_____

_____

_____

Dates valid _____ through _____

Emergency Information

Contact information for contractor or repair person _____

_____

_____

Contact information for contractor or repair person _____

_____

_____

Contact information for contractor or repair person _____

_____

_____

Alternate Key Holders

Name _____

Address _____

_____

Telephone _____

Cell phone _____

Relationship to client _____

Name _____

Address _____

_____

Telephone _____

Cell phone _____

Relationship to client _____

Name _____

Address _____

_____

Telephone _____

Cell phone _____

Relationship to client _____

Telephone and Account Numbers (where applicable)

Gas company _____

_____

_____

Electric company _____

_____

_____

Water bureau _____

_____

_____

Telephone company _____

_____

_____

Fire department _____

_____

_____

Police department _____

_____

_____

Poison control _____

_____

_____

Veterinarian _____

_____

_____

Client_____

Date	Hours	Amt. Due	Date Billed	Invoice #	Date paid	Comments

Invoicing

There are many ways to invoice clients, from an understanding that a check will be left on the kitchen counter every week (be sure to get this agreement in writing) to weekly or monthly statements. You can find invoice forms at office-supply and stationery stores, or purchase software that helps you create your own. Following is a sample invoice that might be helpful.

Colonial Village Cleaners

123 Brownstone Street

Cleveland, Ohio 12345

(123) 555-1234

Invoice number _____

Date _____

Client name and address

_____

_____

_____

_____

Services   **Amount Due**

_____   _____

_____   _____

_____   _____

_____   _____

_____   _____

_____   _____

_____   Total: _____

Payment is due within 14 days.

11 | Taxes

Operating your own business and working for a business are two entirely different experiences. When you work for a company, the only tax issue you need to deal with is ensuring that your state and federal taxes are being withheld at the appropriate rate. When you own a business, however, the mere mention of taxation can be a bit intimidating. Sometimes new business owners fall into the trap of thinking that they don't need to follow business tax regulations. Often, the owner of a start-up will wait to turn a profit before showing this on her or his tax returns. That's a big no-no.

As a self-employed business owner, you'll be paying taxes not once a year but quarterly: Every three months, you'll send both the state and federal governments a check covering your estimated tax bill for that period. The estimates are based on your previous year's income, and at the end of each tax year, you reconcile the estimated payments you made with the actual income you ended up receiving. If you overpaid, you'll get a refund; if you underpaid, you'll send in what you owe. You don't get any bills or statements from the government reminding you of your quarterly tax obligation; it's up to you to send it in, and if you don't, you can face some stiff penalties and nasty surprises come April 15. Your accountant or tax preparer can help you with all of this, and you can also get information from the Small Business Administration or the IRS (see "Appendix II: Resources").

Deductions for the Home-Based Business

In order to be eligible for home-business-related tax deductions, the Internal Revenue Service requires that the specific portion of your home that you are going to claim as a business deduction be used regularly and exclusively for business. This is the principal location of your business or a place you have reserved to meet prospective customers and conduct office administration. The location may not be used to entertain family members or to store personal belongings. Any equipment that you claim, such as a telephone or computer, must also be used exclusively for business purposes.

In order for your business to qualify under the exclusive-use test, you must be using the deductible portion of your home for only business-related activities. This area can be a separate room or other clearly defined area of your home. It does not have to be marked off by a permanent partition of any kind. For instance, let's say that your dining room doubles as a home office. Three or four times a week, you use your dining room as a place to prepare customer billing statements, review contracts, and read industry journals. Your family also uses this room for meals. The dining room is not considered to be an exclusive home office, and therefore it cannot be used to claim a business deduction. In order for your business to qualify under the regular-use test, you must be using a specific area of your home for business on a *regular* basis.

You will not meet the test if the business use of the area is only incidental or occasional, even if you don't use it for any other reason. Suppose you use a specific part of your home, such as a spare bedroom, to regularly view promotional videotapes on stock-market variations, investment strategies, and trends. You don't, however, actually invest in the market or otherwise participate in the opportunities described in the tapes. Because these activities are not part of your regular business function, you cannot claim a business deduction for the business use of your spare room.

As your business grows, you may have other business locations in addition to your home. In order to qualify for a business deduction for the use of your home, you must be able to meet the principal place of business test. Your home office may qualify as your principal place of business for deducting certain expenses if you meet the following criteria:

- You use your home office for administrative or managerial activities for your business exclusively and regularly.
- Your home office is the only fixed area in which you regularly and exclusively conduct substantial administrative or managerial activities.

On the other hand, if you use the home office for your business exclusively and regularly, but your home office does not qualify as your principal location for business based on the above rules, you can establish your principal place of business based on the relative importance of the activities performed and the function served at each location, or the time spent at each location.

If your home office cannot be identified as your principal place of business, you won't be able to claim it as an expense. There may still be other ways for you to deduct home office expenses, however.

If you regularly meet or greet clients or customers in a part of your home throughout the normal course of your business—even though you generally conduct your business at another location or locations—you may be able to deduct expenses for that part of your home. That portion must be used exclusively and regularly for business, and qualifies for a deduction if:

- you actually meet clients or customers on your premises; or
- the use of your home is an integral and substantial part of the way in which you conduct your business.

The occasional use of your home for business meetings and business-related phone calls would not qualify you for a deduction of the expenses for the business part of your home. You may also deduct the expenses for a separate structure, such as a garage or shed, if it's freestanding and you use it for the exclusive and regular use of your business. This structure does not have to be your principal place of business or a place where you meet clients or customers. For example, Albert Jones operates a candle shop in town. He makes the candles in a garage behind his house. Because Mr. Jones only uses the garage exclusively and regularly for his candle-making business, he will be able to deduct the expenses for the use of the garage.

Once you have met the criteria for qualifying for deductions, you can then figure out how much you can deduct. You must determine the percentage of your home used for your business. There are two commonly used methods:

- Divide the area that's used for business (length multiplied by width) by the total area of your home.
- Divide the number of rooms used for your business by the total number of rooms in the house. You can use this method as long as your rooms are all of comparable size.

You won't be able to deduct the business expense of your home office for times when you did not use your home office for business purposes or endeavors. For example, if you set up your home business on July 1, when it comes time to calculate your yearly allowable tax deductions, you must begin in the calendar month that the business was launched—in this case, July. You cannot claim expenses from the beginning of the calendar year.

Remember, the Internal Revenue Service is going to be treating the part of your home that you use for business as though it were a separate entity, a separate piece of property. What this means to the home-business owner is that meticulous records must be kept. There should be no mixing of business and personal receipts. All business receipts and logs need to be kept separate. There is no one method that is required, but your records must clearly justify the deductions that you'll be claiming for your home business. Claiming home-business deductions does not automatically instigate an audit of your tax return. Still, it's always wise to keep thorough records and to stay well within the boundaries set up to qualify for home-business deductions. Consult a tax specialist or other similar expert in this field when managing this particular aspect of your business.

Deductions for the Housecleaning Business

Generally, in order to be eligible for business deductions, you must be engaged in an activity with the intent to make a profit. In order to meet this requirement, your business must show a profit in any two years of a five-year period. You may also take business deductions for such things as supplies, subscriptions to business-related journals and publications, an allowance for the business use of your car, insurance, and other related expenses.

Let's take a look at some common business deductions:

- **Advertising.** These expenses include ads placed in the yellow pages, newspaper ads, and magnetic car signs, as well as the costs of printing flyers and business cards (see chapter 13).
- **Automobile expenses.** You can either deduct your actual automobile expenses or use a standard mileage rate. Both methods require you to keep track of your business mileage.

The **actual-expense method** works like this: First, determine what percentage of your car use is for the business. For example, if you put 12,000 miles on your car last year, and have documented 6,000 miles traveled for your housecleaning business, then 50 percent of your vehicle use was business-related (6,000 ÷ 12,000 = 0.50).

Is part of your home used in connection with your business?

NO

YES

Are you an employee?

NO

YES

Do you work at home for the convenience of your employer?

NO

YES

Do you rent part of your home used for business to your employer?

YES

NO

Is the use regular and exclusive?

NO

YES

Is it your principal place of business?

YES

NO

Do you meet clients or customers in your home?

YES

NO

Is it a separate structure?

NO

YES

Deduction NOT allowed

Deduction allowed

You can now deduct 50 percent of your car expenses from your taxable income. This includes all expenses: license and registration fees, insurance, maintenance, repairs, tolls, parking, and gasoline. (Of course, you will have kept meticulous records of all these expenses, and kept invoices and other documents supporting them; see chapter 10.) This is the more complicated method, but it can add up to a larger deduction.

The **standard mileage method** involves simply documenting how many miles you travel for business purposes, then multiplying this mileage by a standard rate that's announced annually by the IRS. At this writing, the rate was 50.5 cents per mile. If you drove 6,000 miles for business purposes, your deduction would be $3,030 (6,000 x .405). All you need to document in this method is the actual mileage. If you use the standard mileage rate, you cannot deduct auto expenses separately; they're included in the rate.

- **Cellular phone.** If 50 percent or more of your phone usage is for business-related calls, you can elect to fully deduct the business portion of the purchase price in the year the phone was bought. If less than 50 percent of its use is for business, you must instead use straight-line depreciation.
- **Clothing.** Clothing that's required for your business that cannot also be used outside of business hours is deductible as a miscellaneous item deduction. The laundry and cleaning expenses involved for qualified clothing are also deductible. Such articles of clothing would include uniforms, safety shoes, and safety goggles. Jeans, even if used exclusively for your job, are not deductible.
- **Computer expenses.** The business parts of your home computer and any peripheral hardware or software equipment are deductible on Schedule C if you own a sole proprietorship. If the computer was bought for business use, you'll be able to deduct the business portion of the purchase price. If 50 percent or more of the computer usage is for business-related activities, you can elect to fully deduct the business portion of the purchase price in the year the computer was bought. If less than 50 percent of its use is for business, you must instead use straight-line depreciation.
- **Health insurance.** If you are self-employed, you may deduct health insurance payments from your gross income on page one of Form 1040. Check with the IRS or your tax preparer for complete information.

- **Home office.** A deduction for your home office is available for your business if you use a portion of your home according to the criteria described earlier.
- **Internet expenses.** Internet expenses related to your business can be deducted on Schedule C and Schedule A as miscellaneous deductions.
- **Licenses.** Licenses related to your business may be deductible on Schedule C or Schedule A.
- **Subscriptions.** Magazine and trade journal subscriptions, as well as newspapers and books, may be deductible if they're related to your business.
- **Telephone expenses.** Only phone calls that are related to your business, investments, or jobs may be deducted. The cost of a primary phone line isn't deductible, as it's presumed this is for personal use. A second line or a cell phone for business may be deductible, however, along with additional phone services such as call waiting and call forwarding.

Barbara Brown

Rural New England

Barbara Brown has been a home-based housecleaner since 2003. She lives and works in southern Vermont, a rural area where people are spread thin but snow is not. Downhill skiing is a huge draw in her part of the world, where the economy and rhythms of life are heavily influenced by the ski industry. A lot of Barb's business comes from "winter people"—folks who have a second home on or near the slopes, who arrive in droves for the ski season.

It's a family business. Barb has three kids, two of them now young adults. "My daughter and I are the main core of the business these days," she says. It's a busy, thriving concern—so busy that she has a waiting list. "If it comes to crunch time, in winter, we recruit family members. I try not to go outside the family, where it's harder to get the best people. And—smaller is better!

"It's hard to regulate my schedule to get year-round people," Barb admits. "People use their houses in winter only, and when they're here they want cleaning. I'm trying to get a more established, regular clientele. It's been hard, but I'm getting there. Because I have a waiting list, I'm starting to be able to take the cream of the crop for clients." It makes for a frantically busy winter, and slow times the rest of the year.

Barb has advertised on occasion, but the vast majority of her clients come to her via word of mouth. "Word gets around," she says. "People stop me in the grocery store, or they see the sign on my truck when I drive by." She's never felt the need to get a Web site. "In this remote area, it doesn't really work," she explains. "The population is too spread out."

The word on Barb is that she's good. Indeed, "You've got to give it your all," she says. "You can't cut corners. It does take a lot of time. You've got to have it in you to do a really thorough job, not a lick and a promise! You can't do it halfway and get the business. To do a really good job just makes you feel good, too."

She acknowledges, "Green is the way to go. Try to use some of the green products. They don't work the same way, however. It can be frustrating to scrub and scrub and know that all it would take is a squirt of chemical and the job would be done." Still, she says, "Clients really like the green products, and it's hard to breathe chemical fumes all day long. I recommend trying some and seeing how they work for you—finding out which ones you can work in."

With a bit of reluctance, she offers up her favorite trade secret. "When we're all done with something—say a counter in the kitchen or bathroom, or a bathroom sink—we go over it with Pledge. It makes the surface smooth as silk. Even toothpaste doesn't stick. I get all kinds of comments on it. People love it." A little-known way to get professional results that people will comment on, even if it's your very first job!

And a final piece of advice: "Read. I'm always looking for tips in magazines, always looking for something to make my life easier. You can find great ideas all over the place."

12

Insurance and Bonding

In today's lawsuit-happy culture, no business can afford to be uninsured. Likewise, an in-home service provider should carry a surety bond, also known as a dishonesty bond, to cover incidents of theft. Of course, you're not stealing anything yourself, but anyone at any time can claim that a household item is missing and point a finger at anyone with access to the house. You can also be sued for any number of offenses, real or imagined. Therefore, it's critical that you understand how liability and bonding work, to save yourself a lot of anxiety and headaches down the road.

Liability Insurance

Liability insurance is protection for yourself, your income, your home, and any other property that you own should a client slap you with a lawsuit. You might think, *I'm only cleaning houses; what could I possibly be sued for?* The answer is *Quite a bit*. Because you're going into someone's home to provide a service, you can be sued for damage to or theft of any item in that home, as well as damage to the building structure itself. Legal representation can cost more money than you'll make in two years' time, and you still have to pay the legal fees even if you're found not guilty.

The most common lawsuit is for damages to the client's property. The obvious damages to someone's property are usually accidental. Breakage, for instance, is something that happens to the best of us, usually through no fault of our own. Perhaps you go to open a window blind and the entire fixture crashes to the floor, breaking a table lamp in the process. Or maybe a client has crowded glass or ceramic items so tightly together that you break one while trying to pick it up and dust it. During your in-home consultation, you should always carefully evaluate such areas. It could easily take several hours to safely and responsibly clean the items in a china cabinet.

You could also be sued for damages that result from tracking mud or engine grease onto a client's Oriental carpet. Or you might be held responsible for the damages caused by using the wrong products, even if the label stated that the product was suitable for the surface you used it on. Major problems such as structural damage to the building or water and fire damage could be your responsibility. Or suppose you leave a door unlocked and someone comes in and ransacks the place—again, you're up the creek. Seasoned cleaners as well as newcomers to the trade often think, *It won't happen to me.* Never say never!

Over the years we've collected several lawsuit horror stories from other cleaners.

- One cleaner slipped on a child's toy that was on the kitchen floor, accidentally putting a hole in the plaster wall with the handle of the broom she was holding. (Remember, just because something is an accident doesn't mean you're not responsible for the damages.) The client never asked the cleaner to repair the hole in the plaster; he simply slapped her with a suit for close to $10,000, which included replacement of the entire wall. You might think that the presence of the toy on the floor was the client's fault—which it was—but it never occurred to the cleaner to file a countersuit. The client argued that it was less expensive to replace the wall than to patch and paint it. The figure also included the cost of replacing the toy that was damaged when the cleaner stepped on it, as well as compensation for the personal suffering that the client endured by having to look at a wall with a hole in it for a while. He also argued that he used his home for business meetings but was unable to use the room where the damage occurred from the time that the hole appeared until the wall was replaced, a period of six weeks. He claimed business losses, and was awarded the judgment. Fortunately, the cleaner had liability insurance. Although she only had to pay her $250 deductible, that's still a lot of money for something that wasn't really her fault.
- Another cleaner was accused of having left an upstairs bathroom sink faucet running with the sink stopper in place; no one noticed it for a day and a half. The family was alerted when the second floor, which had become

waterlogged, collapsed. The cleaner argued that she'd never even turned on the faucet in that bathroom. She was hit with a $60,000 lawsuit to cover the cost of the repair, as well as temporary housing in a first-class hotel suite for the family from the day the damage occurred until the repair was completed (three months). The last we heard, the case was still in litigation. The lawyer for the cleaner's insurance company brought up a valid point: Within the home resided three children, all under the age of five, who were roaming the house unsupervised during the time that the cleaner was there. This is another reason not to work when unsupervised children or other people are present in the home, and another argument for having liability insurance!

- A cleaner had her purse stolen from her locked car while she was in the local movie theater. The purse contained a key ring with all of her clients' house keys. All eleven of the clients' homes had to be rekeyed, at the cost of nearly $400 per home. The housecleaner had no insurance, and she was not able to pay the incurred charges. Some of the clients are in litigation with their homeowner's insurance providers, and some of those providers have refused to pay. Consequently, the clients have filed suit. This cleaner will eventually have to make restitution to the clients, which she can't afford to do. She has subsequently lost her business and her reputation, a nightmare that could easily have been avoided by purchasing even a minimal liability policy.

Always maintain a liability insurance policy. It's inexpensive, and you'll be known as a reputable service provider. Put yourself in the client's shoes: Would you want an uninsured person coming into your home and handling heirlooms, expensive china, costly crystal, or collectible artwork? Or mopping your $20,000 marble floor with the wrong product? Would you consider going to a medical doctor or auto mechanic who wasn't insured?

On the other hand, you must always be on the alert for people who might try to pull off an insurance scam. It happens every day. That kindly middle-aged mother of four who hired you to help with household chores because she was overwhelmed could be setting you up to take the fall for fictitious damage or theft. Such people make a sizable living from insurance fraud. Like any other criminal, there's no special look to these characters, and often there's no desperate or bizarre motive other than figuring out how to get away with a moneymaking insurance scam.

During your first consultation, be on the alert if someone asks for explicit details about insurance coverage: liability amounts, renewal dates, and so forth. All the information that clients need is contained in your service manual: your policy number and the name and telephone number of the insurance company, so that they may call the company to confirm your coverage.

There are a couple of ways to go about getting liability insurance for your cleaning business. If you already have insurance for a car, or homeowner's or renter's insurance, call the agent who handles those policies. Because you're already a customer, you'll generally be offered a frequent-user or multiple-policy rate, usually 10 to 15 percent off all your policies. You can also do an Internet search for business liability insurance. There are probably 150 to 200 companies that write policies specifically for small businesses. Most of the Web sources have an online form that you fill out and submit, and an agent will contact you via e-mail with a quote. The rates are usually very reasonable. Avoid giving out your telephone number for insurance quotes: Salespeople pitching the latest insurance plan will bombard you.

Insurance rates differ depending on the state, county, town, township, or city that you live in. The following sample outlines a very basic general liability policy:

Sample Certificate Limits of Liability

$1,000,000	Each occurrence
$2,000,000	General aggregate limit
$1,000,000	Product/completed operations limit
$1,000,000	Personal and advertising injury limit
$50,000	Fire damage limit
$5,000	Medical payments
$10,000	Care, custody, and control
$10,000	Key loss
Deductible:	$250 bodily injury/property damage deductible per claim (including loss adjustment expense)

Before we move on and discuss bonding, let's break down the legal language.

Each Occurrence

An occurrence is each single claim or loss. If a person tries to sue you, the most your insurance company would pay is $1 million—highly unlikely unless you've wreaked total disaster on a million-dollar mansion.

General Aggregate Limit

The general aggregate is the maximum amount of losses that the insurance company will cover during the policy period. In the example shown, the insurance company would pay no more than $2 million during the policy period. (Usually a policy period is one year from the date that you requested and paid for the policy.) If this is part of the policy you purchase, two people at two separate residences could sue you for a million dollars each, or four people could sue you for $500,000 each. In any case, once you hit the $2 million point for one policy year, the insurance company would pay no more. Again, being sued for millions by several people is highly unlikely.

Product/Completed Operations Limit

This coverage isn't really helpful to cleaners, but it's part of any standard liability policy. It simply offers protection from lawsuits that stem from anything you sell or give to your clients. Say, for instance, that you invent a new all-purpose cleaner. You give the product to a client to try, and when she uses it on a glass tabletop, the product chemically reacts with the old product's residue. The new product ignites, starting a fire that damages everything in the room. You'd have plenty of coverage for such an episode. Obviously, you should never give or sell products as part of your cleaning service. Products that you bring to the client's home to use are different (they would be covered as damages) from those you give a client to use.

Personal and Advertising Injury Limit

Advertising injury involves making a statement in your advertising that leads to loss by another person or business through libel, slander, defamation, the violation of the right to privacy, theft of ideas, or infringement of copyright, trademark, title, or slogan. Personal injury, in this case, refers to injuries (damage) that the other person or company claims as a result of your alleged violation. This sort of lawsuit might be filed if you lift ideas, logos, ad copy, and so forth from another person's advertising forum, or if you slander another company and the company loses business because of your comment.

Fire Damage and Medical Payments

These are pretty self-explanatory. If you cause a fire, the general policy will cover up to $50,000 in damage. Fires are rare; as a housecleaner, you shouldn't have any reason to light a flame. After all, you're cleaning, not cooking. A medical-payments clause would cover a client for injury suffered—for instance, a client who's hurt when attempting to use your homemade cleaning product, or one who stops by your home to drop off your check and slips on the ice on the sidewalk. You've got $5,000 worth of medical coverage to use for such a client. This is medical coverage for other people who are physically hurt or injured as a result of your negligence; it is not medical coverage for you. In the case of a serious injury that might cost more than $5,000, the client is covered under her or his medical and/or homeowner's insurance; that's why the general coverage is low. If you're worried about this, you can purchase additional coverage for a small fee.

Care, Custody, and Control

This is part of the general liability policy that is infrequently used. It covers property that is temporarily placed in your possession. *Temporarily* is the key word. If you agreed to care for a rare plant for a client who was planning a lengthy vacation, for instance, and the plant died, you'd be covered. Still, you won't have to worry about this clause if you set boundaries with your clients. Accept no other duty or responsibility other than the housecleaning work that you contracted to do.

Key Loss

If you ever lose a client's keys, this clause will be your saving grace. To avoid having to fall back on this coverage, follow responsible security standards by locking all keys in a safe when they're not in use.

Do you see how you can get burned by giving in to requests for work that has nothing to do with housecleaning? You might simply agree to turn on the teakettle and end up with a million-dollar lawsuit. As we've pointed out in previous sections of this book, always think carefully about accepting a job if the client or other people are going to be in the house. Someone could easily trip over the electric cord to the vacuum cleaner (the cord that you plugged in), break a leg, and then sue you for negligence. It happens every day, and you can't afford to think it can't happen to you.

Bonding

General liability policies don't cover theft; for this, you need to purchase a surety bond. These are inexpensive—around $50 per $5,000 of coverage—and are good for one year. The bond covers litigation costs and the value of the stolen item (up to the amount of the bond purchased) if you are convicted of the crime. A client can accuse you of stealing a $20,000 Rolex watch from his jewelry box, for instance, but not much will come out of such an accusation unless he can prove it. He'd need to have some pretty incriminating evidence, or a reliable witness to the crime. Without these, he'd have to present a case built on circumstantial evidence.

If an item turns up missing, you cannot be convicted simply because you were in the home, or because you have a key to the house. These sorts of claims rarely go anywhere because theft is very difficult to prove. Still, paying the $50 bond fee is worth the money because it sends out the message that you are a professional who does not take risks. Bonding is the mark of a reputable business. It also dissuades scam artists from making fraudulent claims.

Surety bonds are available through most insurance companies. If the provider of your liability policy doesn't offer these bonds, your agent should be able to refer you to a firm that does. There are also dozens of bond providers that advertise on the Internet. If you conduct a search, however, be sure to use the term *surety bond*; otherwise, you'll get a list of thousands of people who provide bail bonds (to spring people out of jail), which have nothing to do with surety bonds.

It's fairly easy to secure a bond. The form asks for basic information: name of the company, address, and so forth. It also asks if you've been convicted of a crime within the past seven years. If you have been convicted, answer truthfully. A *yes* answer doesn't mean automatic denial, especially if you were convicted of something minor, such as not paying parking tickets. If you are unable to be bonded because of a criminal conviction, there isn't much you can do except shop around. Some bonding companies will take the risk; others won't.

If at some point you decide to hire an independent contractor to work for your company, you will need to purchase liability coverage for that person. This changes your policy from that of a sole proprietor to a standard policyholder, and the rates will increase by about 60 percent. You will also need to purchase a surety bond for each employee. Most sole-proprietor insurance policies and bonds will automatically extend to include a spouse, free of charge, but neither the policy nor the bond covers anyone else.

If you advertise your company as being insured and bonded, be sure to keep the coverage up-to-date. The last thing you need is a lawsuit and an expired policy. If you feel that the general liability policies have inadequate limits, you can purchase additional limits for a small fee. If you do in fact work in an area where homes are valued at $25 million—Beverly Hills, Bel-Air, Palm Springs—it won't hurt you to up your coverage.

Zen Home Cleaning

New York City
www.zenhomecleaning.com

With a motto of "Luxury Green Home Therapy Services," Zen Home is not your average cleaning company. It was the first firm in New York City to go green, according to founder-owner Deanna Hains. Phenomenally successful virtually since its inception, Zen provides luxe cleaning services, is 100 percent green in every aspect of its business (right down to the floor stain in its offices), and even offers home-organizing, eco-painting, and feng shui services to clients.

"We're three years old now, and we're expanding," says Deanna. "We've had a lot of growth really fast." She started the business from her own home, "just like almost everyone else did. Once you find a few clients, you can very easily work from your home. Start-up costs are nominal. You're not paying for office space." Deanna enlisted the help of a friend whom she'd worked with before—"I knew her, she was a great person. I really trusted her." She placed ads in local newspapers and on Craigslist, bought some cleaning products at local grocery stores . . . and a business was born.

Sounds easy, but Deanna had one more crucial ingredient: a vision. "The home is special—a haven. Appreciation for the home is really important to me." A big part of this focus is committing to using only healthy products in the home—healthy for people, for pets, for plants, for the planet. "Green is a part of my life. I've been a vegan for sixteen years. I used nontoxic products for years before starting the business." The desire to make home a welcoming place for stressed-out city dwellers struck an immediate chord with clients.

And then serendipity happened. Among those first clients was an editor at *DailyCandy*—a daily online newsletter that collects tidbits about exciting new products, services, and events in New York City. It goes out to thousands of people across the metro area. The editor so appreciated his Zen cleaning that he gave the firm a mention in the October 2005 issue of *DailyCandy*.

"Everything changed," says Deanna. "We got 300 calls and 300 e-mails *that day.*" Most were from wannabe customers, but many were from other folks in the media, who frequently rely on *DailyCandy* for tips. A cascade of publicity followed; Zen Home was written up in *New York* magazine, *Wall Street Journal, Domino* magazine, *TimeOut New York, Apartment Therapy,* and more.

It's not a typical business trajectory. Yet when you match an authentic, passionate belief in your work with great timing, great follow-through, and energy that doesn't quit—well, clearly, this kind of success *can* happen.

It's not without a downside, though. "For a while," says Deanna, "We had more clients than we had cleaners. It sounds like a great problem to have, but it's not. You end up turning away money! It can overwhelm you, and service can suffer."

Zen Home created a waiting list and began hiring in earnest. That process brings pitfalls of its own. "You have to find people who are reliable—it's a big issue in this business. Housecleaning isn't the most glamorous job, and people don't tend to hold it in high regard. Turnover is high. Employees try it for a while and then quit. And as the owner, you have to be able to devote the time and be there yourself if one of your employees isn't available."

The learning curve was steep, but Deanna handled it. "We've finally gotten to a point where we've got a great staff, a lot of cleaners who work for us. We're at a really good level now. It happened for us."

One of the secrets for Zen has been devoting as much time, commitment, and energy to happy *employees* as happy clients. "There's a lack of respect out there for housecleaners," Deanna notes. "It's not right. These are the people cleaning your toilets, picking up your dirty laundry—there should be a *lot* of respect for that! So we do everything we can to glamorize this position. We have beautiful uniforms for our cleaners. We spend a lot of time educating our employees—we hold seminars every month on things like healthy nutrition, wellness, ways to be ecologically friendly.

"One of my greatest pleasures in this business," she continues, "is going into a home and seeing our employees do a great job. Our cleaners organize so well! We want clients *and* employees to feel good about what we're doing. We want our employees to take real pride in themselves."

Personnel issues are ongoing in any business, of course. Once you've taken on even a single employee, a whole new level of business challenges kick in. "You have to have workers' comp first of all," Deanna stresses. "Even with one person, you have to have it. Second: Make sure you have general liability insurance. When I started, I didn't have it immediately—it's expensive—but I had only two employees. You're sending employees into clients' homes, so be sure to hire people you really trust. Remember, whether you have insurance or not, if someone steals something you may have to pay for it."

The honesty issue comes into play on both sides, too: "Employee *or* client. If clients lose something and a cleaning service was there, the first thing they do is assume the cleaner stole it." Take the time to learn about the insurance policies available to you, she advises. It's not an easy task, but it can make or break a business. "Protect yourself."

Going green has been crucial to Zen's success as well. "It's a lot easier now," says Deanna. "Green wasn't popular three years ago! Also, it's not just about buying cleaning products. You have to do the research—you have to know *why* you want green products. Be knowledgeable about not just cleaning but what's happening on the planet as well."

Zen's green commitment extends into every aspect of the business. "We don't use paper towels at all. We use microfiber cloths and wash them every day," Hains says.

"And we have a dispenser system. Our cleaning consultants come into the office every morning, fill up their containers from our supplies, and take them with them to their appointments. They use the same bottles again and again. When we set up the offices here, we only used nontoxic paint, nontoxic floor stain. We have a watercooler but no plastic cups; we use cups made of recycled materials and wash them every day. Green is a hot trend these days, and a lot of folks are capitalizing on it simply as a way to make money." Zen Home, on the other hand, walks the talk, and it shows. "Try to get as much information as you can *before* you start," Deanna suggests.

Another cornerstone of Zen's services is luxury. These cleaners don't just slog through a list of basics and go home; they go the extra mile to make each home a refuge, a place of beauty and peace. "We base our cleaning on five-star hotel services," says Deanna. "We use hotel corners when we make the beds. We add triangle folds to the toilet paper. Really special things." They also burn the essential oils of your choice while they work, then leave organic chocolates on your pillow at the end of the day. "It really makes people feel good when they go home. Everybody has stress. We want clients to go home at the end of the day and find that the energy of their home has been completely transformed because Zen Home has been there.

"I am so happy to have this business," Deanna concludes. "There are so many pleasures owning Zen Home. It's hard work, but I like it so much. It's not purely to make money. One of my models has always been running the company by the books, doing the right thing. It's worked well."

It sure has. Zen Home Cleaning, which began with one woman, an idea, and a home office, now employs more than thirty people and is in the process of expanding across the country—creating a cleaner, more serene world, one city at a time.

13 Marketing

Marketing is the most important component of building a profitable business. Still, with so many choices available for new businesses, it's hard to know where to start and how much money to set aside for ads, for example. You could spend as little as $10 or as much as $1,500 and get the same results. Marketing for a one-person cleaning business is far different from the strategy that an operation with fifteen employees would use. It isn't worth your while—at least not at first—to invest in a huge, expensive advertising package.

To develop an effective marketing strategy, you need a pretty good idea of your expected business growth. Many cleaners are satisfied with operating a one-person business and want nothing to do with hiring employees or serving hundreds of clients. There's nothing wrong with such a choice; in fact, this is how the majority of cleaning businesses prefer to operate. On the other hand, a few owners are interested in immediate growth, expansion of services, and higher profits. Either choice will affect how you go about choosing advertising forums.

For now, let's assume that your company will function with you as the sole employee. Because there's only so much business that you can accommodate, it doesn't make much sense to spend an entire year's projected salary on an advertising package that will generate more business than you can handle. Turning away hordes of potential clients will only cause aggravation, both for you and for the folks inquiring about services.

What sort of marketing works best? Let's take a closer look at your choices.

The Internet

The Internet is your best selling tool. It's inexpensive and delivers up-to-the-minute information. Today's consumers are Web-savvy, and a vast majority of American households have computers. Getting a Web site is easy: If your Internet service provider (ISP) provides a free home page, your site can be up and running within twenty-four hours. The Web site can answer almost any question that potential customers might have before they even pick up the phone.

To set up a Web site of your own, begin by registering your domain name. On a search engine, type in "domain name" or "domain registration"; you'll get thousands of possibilities. Look through ten or twenty of them and compare prices. Three of the most popular domain registries that have been around for quite a while are:

- www.registernames.com
- www.ICDomainnames.com
- www.networksolutions.com

Because the domain registries are competing against each other, they try to come up with a variety of package plans, discounts, and specials. At times these options can be as confusing as choosing a long-distance telephone provider. The basic plan includes simply the use of the domain name and Web forwarding; this is all you really need. The total price for a one-year package often runs less than $100. You're then ready to set up your Web site. If your ISP offers free home pages, you're

Melinda's Story

Since I developed and launched my Web site, I haven't had to run a single newspaper ad. The site is linked to my ISP home page; I pay a small yearly fee for my domain name and a Web forwarding function. The Web page lists my zones and services. If customers like what they see, they can download my service guide to read and review it. Then they can e-mail or phone me for further information or to set up a consultation. It's a great way to do business: You weed out the folks who aren't willing to pay your rates, and the frequently asked questions are answered before you even pick up the phone. And you can't beat the cost! I'd estimate that 95 percent of my new customers come to me as a result of my Web presence.

in business. AOL has a user-friendly Web page building tool called Hometown; other ISPs have similar features.

If you don't like the Web tools available through your ISP, or if the provider charges you for home pages, you can still build a free Web site. There are many companies on the Web that provide free pages. All of them come with advertising in the form of pop-ups, clickable icons, banners, and so on. Compare the sites to see which is the least annoying to you and—more importantly—to your customers. Here are some recommended Web page providers:

- http://geocities.yahoo.com
- www.angelfire.lycos.com
- www.hypermart.com
- www.tripod.lycos.com
- www.godaddy.com

Your Web site itself should be clean, clutter-free, professional, and easy to navigate and maintain. The simplest structure to use is a three-page site. This gives you enough space to describe your business without clutter. The first page, the home page, will give basic information: company name, mission statement, the geographic area you serve, and an icon that people can click to read about your services. The second page, Services, provides a brief description of what you offer as well as an opportunity to request your Guide to Services. Be sure to include your phone number and an e-mail address for people to contact.

The third page, a photo gallery, gives potential clients a visual sampling of your work. You can find stock photos of clean houses to use, but they tend to look like, well, stock photos. A better choice is real clients' homes—with their permission, of course. A photo of yourself, if you're comfortable with that, puts a human face on your company and can be a strong selling point. You're asking potential clients to invite a stranger into their homes; visual images make that process much less nerve-racking for them.

Likewise, write the copy you use yourself rather than using templates or adapting other people's text. Your cleaning company is unique, a reflection of your skills, values, and hard work. Generic copy, on the other hand, is easy to spot, and it sends the message that you have nothing to say about your business.

Make a point of including the terms that potential customers will be searching for as they cruise the Web: *cleaner, housecleaner,* and your geographic area, along with any specialty you may have: green, organic, luxury, antiques, and so on. You want to make sure that when people enter, say, "green housecleaner Phoenix" into a search engine, your site will be listed among the responses.

This is indeed the age of the Internet. Your kids have their own Web sites; your clients do, your neighbors do, and so does your six-year-old niece, along with her hamster. Can you afford *not* to be on the Web?

Yellow Pages

The local Yellow Pages work well for large corporations but not so well for small businesses. Typical Yellow Pages listings can cost from hundreds to thousands of dollars per year. The larger the city or town, the higher the fee. It simply isn't worth the yearly gain of two or three clients. Furthermore, what happens once your business takes off and your time slots are filled? There your Yellow Page ad will sit, attracting new customers whom you'll have to disappoint.

Newspapers

Newspapers are by far one of the least expensive and most effective ways of getting the word out. Because you're a small company that serves a specific locale, an ad in the smallest community paper of that area will start the ball rolling. Be sure to limit your ads to those newspapers serving the zones you actually work in!

Display Ads

Display ads are far better than classified ads. People are much more apt to notice and remember display ads than text. You don't need fancy graphics; your simple black-on-white business card will be just fine. Before you purchase a display ad, leaf through the newspaper and select two or three sections where you'd like your ad inserted. Newspapers will charge a small additional fee if you request that your ad be placed in a specific section of the paper. It's worth it. A display ad placed in the family section, among ads for children's activities and day-care services, is likely to generate much more business than one placed next to advertisements for funeral homes and florists.

Classified Ads

Classified ads are becoming a thing of the past. They can be very expensive; some periodicals charge several dollars a word, with a twenty-five-word minimum. They generate less business now than they did years ago, simply because of the increase in Web shopping. You could, however, gain clients rather inexpensively by placing a carefully worded classified ad in a community newspaper. We don't recommend placing advertising in those small weekly publications that are geared exclusively toward classifieds. We don't know of any housecleaners who have had an ounce of luck with them, and you probably won't either; the people who read them are usually in the market for cars or furniture, not household services. Save your money to advertise in a regular newspaper.

Online Classifieds

Craigslist is perhaps the best known among the growing numbers of free online classified ads out there. Type "online classified" and your area into any search engine and start looking. These ads are free, more and more people are turning to them every day—and did we mention that they're free? You may or may not have anything to gain from posting an ad, but you certainly don't have anything to lose.

Flyers

Flyers can be tempting: They're relatively easy and inexpensive to produce, and can be distributed quickly and easily. In truth, however, more people will throw them away than will actually read them. Let's see what works and what doesn't.

If you're like most people, you've probably received dozens of flyers on your car windshield over the years, and you've probably been more angered than interested. Many homes have a NO SOLICITATION sign on the door or a decal that states NO HANDBILLS OR FLYERS. If you ignore the resident's wishes, you could be issued a citation. This is especially true in apartment and condo buildings, which often have strict rules against solicitation. It's also against federal law to place anything in a mailbox.

One solution is the doorknob hanger. Blank doorknob hangers can be purchased in office supply stores for around 50 cents apiece. They're made of thick card stock and are far more attractive than mass-photocopied flyers. You can print them on your home computer and be selective about where you hang them. For instance, wherever you see a moving truck or a HOUSE FOR SALE sign, place a hanger on the doorknob. Folks just moving into a neighborhood will likely be interested in the services available in their new community. Furthermore, someone who is moving out may need help cleaning the home and preparing it for the new tenant. Keep your eye out for new housing developments. They are prime candidates! You could feasibly sign up an entire neighborhood in a week's time.

Business Cards

Never leave home without one!

Anytime you have reason to mention your occupation, take advantage of the opportunity to hand out a business card. Did you know that within a twenty-four-hour period, you probably mention your occupation at least seven times? And think about all the community bulletin boards you see in your daily life. Each one is free advertising! Take advantage especially of bulletin boards located where busy people convene or are running errands:

- supermarkets and health-food stores
- gyms and weight-loss centers
- schools and community centers
- hospitals (people recovering from surgery or childbirth might desperately need your services!)

- libraries
- veterinary offices
- churches
- day spas
- senior centers

Busy, active people are all potential clients. Whenever you can, you want to place a business card either in the hands of these people or at eye level in the places they frequent.

Business cards are inexpensive. You can have them professionally printed by an offset printing house by the thousands for about $200. The simplest and least expensive business card to produce is one that includes a simple black-on-white logo, a one-sentence motto or affirmation, and your telephone number or Web address. If you choose to include colors, you'll be paying more: Expect the price to go up at least $175 per color for each 1,000 cards.

Most printers will print a run of 1,000 cards with a one-time setup fee of about $50. The setup fee is charged because the printer has to make a plate of your card—something like a large metal mold. The plate is stored with the printing house; anytime you need more cards, the plate is pulled and the cards printed. Be aware, though, that some printers have a minimum print run of 5,000 cards or more. Many printing houses on the Internet advertise incredibly inexpensive print runs. You'll want to look at these carefully; when you factor in the postage, the cost often exceeds what the printer down the street might charge. Large print runs can set you back around $1,000 if you don't shop around.

You can also buy sheets of blank business cards to print from your home computer. Blank cards are available at office-supply stores in packages of 100 to 500. A 100-card package costs about $15, and the business card software can run anywhere from $10 to $50. There are advantages and disadvantages to printing your own cards. On the plus side, it's far less expensive than commercial printing if you have a simple logo. CD-ROM storage allows you to upload the logo image to the business card software. You can have your cards printed and ready to go in about thirty minutes. Even the no-frills, least-complicated business card software includes a hefty selection of font and print styles to choose from. The higher-end software contains hundreds of styles. You can choose to print the cards all at once or only as needed. You can also experiment with different card designs: vertical or horizontal logo placement, bold text, and so forth. You're not bound to any one design: If you don't like what you've developed, you can change it and create a totally different card in less than ten minutes.

The downside is that if you use colors, you'll go through ink cartridges quickly, and color cartridges are expensive. Also, although the cards are perforated for easy separation, you've got to be careful. If you pull too hard, you can easily damage the cards, resulting in waste.

Magnetic Car Signs

I like to think of magnetic car signs as business cards for cars! They're inexpensive head turners. Magnetic car signs, which can be made by a multifunctional printer, usually come in pairs (one for the driver's side door and one for the passenger's side) and cost between $50 and $100. There are many graphic artists who specialize in magnetic signs and who advertise on the Internet. The most economical and useful sign is simply text on a white background. You need only the name of your business, perhaps a short phrase such as HOUSECLEANING BY APPOINTMENT, and your Web address or telephone number.

Make sure the signs are on your car at all times, and especially when you're parked in high-traffic areas such as supermarket parking lots. When you're parked at clients' homes, too, neighbors will take notice. You'll be amazed not only at the number of inquiries but also at how many of those inquiries turn into jobs! Because the signs are magnetic, they're easy to remove anytime you prefer not to display them.

Networking

Networking is the oldest form of advertising. Centuries ago, proprietors advertised via word of mouth only; there were no phone books or newspapers. Today, despite mass media, community networking remains a resourceful and reliable plan for getting the word out about your business. And it's free! To be included in a network of service providers is an honor that must be earned, so don't be surprised if it takes several months to start making connections. To make it easier, be the first to approach other professional service providers. Such folks can include:

- wedding planners
- pet-sitters

- interior decorators
- child-care providers
- lawn-care workers
- visiting nurses and home health-care aides
- errand-running services

E-mail or telephone the other provider and explain a little bit about your company: the types of clients you serve, your zones of service, availability, a rough example of rates, and so forth. Ask if you can exchange flyers or business cards. Have a large index card available to write down contact information about the other provider and her or his company. Offer to recommend the provider's services should you ever receive an inquiry, and ask the other provider to do the same. Clients usually feel better about hiring someone based on a personal referral. As a housecleaner, then, the next time you're asked about lawn mowing, you can go to your file and pull out the name, Web address, or phone number of someone who provides that service. Clients will be thrilled, and you will be, too, when other providers offer your name to folks inquiring about housecleaning services.

Word of Mouth

The very best advertising is free—and it's priceless. If you do good work, your own clients will sell your services for you. There are housecleaners out there who have never advertised in any way. One client told a friend . . . who told a friend . . . who told a friend . . . and soon the cleaners had waiting lists. Provide superior service, and the world will come to you!

It may come slowly, of course. Word of mouth, more than any other marketing method, takes time. Be patient. You have everything to gain.

Fund-Raising and Community Outreach

Get involved in your community by donating your time and services at least once a month. Not only is volunteering a great humanitarian effort, but it's also fun and a great way to advertise for free. Find a cause that you're interested in. If time is an issue for you, you can make a small monetary contribution in the name of your business. It's tax deductible, and the charity will be grateful. Here are some examples of creative volunteering:

- Help sponsor community events: blood drives, walkathons, car washes, pet

Medium	Cost	Effectiveness	Comments
The Internet	Low-cost: $30–$50 per month	Extremely effective	Highly recommended. It's possible to generate almost all of your business through the Internet
Yellow Pages	Expensive: $700–$3,000 per year	Not effective	Chances are you won't get clients when you want them, and you'll get too many when you don't.
Newspaper display ad	Low-cost	Very effective	Pay attention to your ad's placement if you want it to be effective.
Classified ad	Fairly expensive: $50–$150 per ad	Somewhat effective	Be as specific about your services as possible for the best response.
Online classified ad	Free	Somewhat effective	Effectiveness varies by region, but it's becoming more and more popular—and you've little to lose.
Flyers	Relatively inexpensive	Somewhat effective	For best results, target your flyers. People buying or selling a home make good candidates. Flyers broadcast indiscriminately get little response.
Business cards	Low-cost to fairly expensive	Very effective	Don't leave home without them!
Magnetic car sign	Low-cost: $50–$100	Very effective	Business cards for cars.
Networking	Free	Very effective	Having a network of service providers to recommend to your clients benefits everyone—and it's free.
Community outreach	Free	Very effective	Generate both new clients and goodwill for your business, and do something worthwhile for your community, too.

adoptions. The name of your business will appear in a newsletter or on television, or it will be posted in a public area.

- Donate your services to a nursing home, hospice, library, or shelter. You'll be helping needy folks, and the employees and coordinators of the institutions will come to see you as an honorable person representing a terrific business—and will likely recommend your services to others.

- Donate a small amount to public television or radio station fund-raisers. They always mention the names of contributors on the air.

- Donate your services to fund-raising auctions. As part of a fund-raising auction for a local women's shelter, one housecleaner donated two hours of cleaning, which was purchased for $450! At the time, two hours of cleaning was a $45 value, so the women's shelter received $450, the benefactor got a clean house, and the cleaner got a $45 tax deduction and referrals to several new clients.

- Organize your own event. Get together with other service providers and pick up trash in a schoolyard or public park. Call the local newspapers to come out and interview you and take photographs.

No matter how little or how much you give, you can't lose when you help charitable causes.

14 When Bad Things Happen to Good Housecleaners

Here's a secret not many people want to talk about: There are some scary people out there. As a housecleaner, you're going to meet some of them. At some point in your career, you may find yourself frustrated, angry, insulted, even downright shocked. It's an occupational hazard. This section is about how to keep your sanity, hold your head up, soar with dignity, and handle the scary situations.

Inappropriate Behavior

How do you know when a prospective or present client is behaving inappropriately? How do you recognize on-the-job stress? What do you do about it?

Inappropriate behavior or abuse can be either overt or covert. Overt is the easier to recognize. It may take the form of yelling; of any sort of physical gesture, including slamming doors, snapping fingers, or shoving; or of chastising you for drinking water or using the bathroom. It's any behavior that humiliates you, and you will recognize it instantly.

Covert abuse is more subtle, and the dividing lines are fuzzier. Is it abusive when someone conducts an inappropriate conversation with family members while you're in the home: yelling at a child, screaming at a spouse, scolding others, including other service providers or employees? How about someone who pumps you for personal information? ("Are you on welfare? What's your religion?") Or a client who refers to you as "the help" or "the girl"? Asks personal questions about other clients? Makes racist, sexist, or otherwise offensive remarks?

Ultimately, these are questions you'll have to answer for yourself. We can tell you this: Pay attention to your instincts. Any behavior that makes you feel uncomfortable deserves a very close look.

So what do you do when faced with an uncomfortable situation, overt or covert? After all, you can't very well tell people how to behave in their own homes. What you *can* do is to remember that you are first and foremost a human being. Second, you are a professional, and as a self-employed professional, you don't have the luxury of reporting inappropriate behavior to higher-ups. You are your own Division of Human Resources, and you must deal with the problem directly.

When things go awry, get out of the situation immediately. Pretending that it doesn't bother you or feeling that you have to put up with poor treatment only perpetuates it. Don't allow second chances for people who degrade you. There is no job worth being humiliated for.

After you've left the situation—walked off the job—let the person know that you've done so because you refuse to tolerate the behavior or comments. It's not always safe to do this face-to-face; you never know what the other person is going to do. You don't want to end up with a mop thrown at you, or worse. Once you're out of there, however, you can write a short note that details why you left, and mail it to the client. You're not going to change anyone's beliefs or prejudices overnight, but you've at least done the right thing by sending out the message that such behavior is unacceptable.

It's important to structure every housecleaning in detail, right from the beginning. Remember the service manual and room plans from chapter 4? These take a long time to complete, but they're critical. They let everyone know what to expect from you.

College professors often spend the first day of each class handing out and reviewing the course syllabus, the key to passing the class. The syllabus lists what is expected and what will happen if the work is not completed at the scheduled time. It includes due dates for reading assignments, quiz and test schedules, presentation dates, and grading criteria. Studying and following the syllabus almost guarantees a high grade. Your service manual and room plans are the syllabus of your housecleaning business.

Structuring every detail of a housecleaning is a lengthy process, but an investment well worth the time. Your manual can save you from some pretty scary situations and people. If a client is put off by your structure, then you're not the right service provider for her or him. You are responsible for maintaining your dignity, self-esteem, and sense of worth. No one can give you dignity, but they can certainly take it away. Choose assignments that will enable you to be valued and rewarded for doing a good job. Remember, you're not just a service provider but also the service regulator. You're in the driver's seat!

Have a Plan

- What will you do if you get sick, or someone in your family does? Have a plan ready just in case. Have contact information readily available.
- What will you do if you fall ill or are injured on the job? Know how to find emergency care near each client's home. Have a plan ready for how you'll get there.
- What will you do if a client—or a client's family member or pet—is sick or injured while you're on the job? Have contact information available, and have a plan ready.
- How will you handle being late for a cleaning appointment? It happens, for any number of reasons, many of them entirely out of your control. Will you stay later than usual? Reduce your fee? Make up the time some other way? If your client is at home expecting your arrival, how will you get in touch?
- What will you do if you inadvertently break or damage something in a client's home? Know what your insurance policy will and won't cover, and who to contact. Think through the process you'll use to tell your client of the problem. See chapter 12, "Insurance and Bonding," for more information.
- What will you do if there's a bad storm or disaster while you're at work? Depending on where you live and work, you can virtually count on lightning, blizzards, earthquakes, floods, tornadoes, hurricanes, or what-have-you occurring at some point in your cleaning career. No, you can't think through every possible emergency, but you can at least envision the possibility and have some ideas about ways to cope.

And that's the point of this sidebar—not to scare the living daylights out of you, but to encourage you to think about bad or exceptional stuff in advance, when your judgment is still clear and you have time to gather the resources and information you might need. A little advance planning will let you relax and enjoy the business you've built for yourself!

First Aid

Cleaning is an active job. You're on your feet, moving, bending, stretching, lifting all day long. Most of the time the worst that will happen is soreness or maybe a bump or bruise. Still, sometimes minor injuries or problems come up. It's a good idea to have a small first-aid kit with you as you clean. This is something you can keep in your vehicle, rather than your cleaning caddy. You won't need it much, but you do want to have ready access.

What to include? Well, you can buy prepacked first-aid kits at drugstores, and chances are these will have everything you need. If you're creating your own, here are some items to think about:

- **Pain relievers.** Aspirin, acetaminophen, ibuprofen, herbal remedies—whatever works for you.
- **Medications.** Have a small supply of any prescription or nonprescription medications you depend on.
- **Bandages.** Even if a cut is tiny, it can still leave drops of blood behind—and bloodstains. So bring bandages in a variety of sizes and shapes. Those strips that come specially designed for knuckles and fingertips are particularly useful.

The Victorian Housekeeper

A century ago, many servants accompanied their employers when they traveled between residences, but the housekeeper generally stayed at the main house, overseeing the order and the overall cleanliness of the household and keeping it in a state of readiness for the employers' return. She was also responsible for all linen (except the table linen), and the estate or house stores: sugar, flour, spices, soaps, and candles. The housekeeper was also charged with keeping the premises free from both rot and vermin. Some made distilled waters from rose, lavender, or lilac, along with soaps and basic medicines for the household's use. Finally, the housekeeper oversaw the yearly spring cleaning, when the house was scrubbed from top to bottom.

- **Disinfectant.** Hydrogen peroxide, rubbing alcohol, or a commercial disinfecting solution. Premoistened disinfectant towelettes are handy.
- **Antibiotic cream or ointment.**
- **Tweezers.**
- **Scissors.**
- **Safety pins.**
- A pair or two of **latex gloves.**
- A list of **contact numbers:** health-care providers, family members, and clients.

You'll no doubt have some of these materials with you as part of your cleaning supplies, but it's useful to set some aside for first-aid purposes, too.

And there are a few more items that—while they don't exactly fall under the heading of "First Aid"—can be mighty helpful to have along. Think about carrying these with you:

- flashlight with extra batteries
- blanket
- cell phone
- eyeglasses repair kit or contact lens solution/spares
- extra clothing: T-shirts, sweatshirts, sweatpants, socks, cleaning apron, what-have-you (in case your own get wet or dirty!)

15 | The Future

Your housecleaning business is limited only by your own imagination. Once you've established yourself and your reputation, you can take your career anywhere you want to go!

Becoming an Employer

If your waiting list is longer than your client list, or if you're simply longing for new challenges, it may be time to expand your business by taking on employees. Becoming an employer is an enormous sea change in your business, and not something to consider lightly. It's also a far larger subject than can be dealt with thoroughly in a volume like this.

If you have employees, you must know and adhere to all the laws and regulations governing employers, including the Equal Employment Opportunity Act, National Labor Relations Act, Age Discrimination in Employment Act, Americans with Disabilities Act, Drug Free Workplace Act, and many others. You also need to know and adhere to all IRS regulations governing employers. This includes verifying each employee's eligibility to work, withholding taxes from her or his paycheck, and keeping on top of all IRS-required paperwork.

Before you hire your first employee, you'll also want to answer these questions:

- What hours will your employee(s) work? What vacation days will you offer? What about sick and/or personal days?
- How much will you pay your employees? How often will you review their work and offer promotions or raises? What criteria will you use to evaluate employees' work?

- What benefits will you offer—health insurance, pension plans, tuition assistance?
- How will you deal with grievances? With employee discipline?
- What will be your policy regarding substance abuse? Sexual harassment?
- What other personnel policies are important to you? Think, for instance, about clothing, eating or smoking on the job, tardiness, confidential information (relating to either clients or your business), use of business or clients' resources for personal activities, and so forth.

You'll also have to deal with recruiting potential employees, interviewing them (this includes complying with all laws and regulations governing nondiscrimination in hiring—for instance, you can't ask a potential employee her or his age or marital status), training them, and sometimes firing them.

And these are just some of the issues you'll have to consider. Clearly, taking on employees can be a full-time job in itself. But if you love dealing with people, have a hearty appetite for administrative work, and have dreams for your business that extend beyond supporting yourself, it offers many challenges and rewards. If you're interested, a great first step is to talk to the people at the Small Business Administration (see "Appendix II: Resources").

There are also some books available that focus on starting and running a staffed cleaning-services business. If your interests lie more in administering a business than in the cleaning itself, these volumes have loads of information:

Aslett, Don A., and Mark L. Browning. *Cleaning Up for a Living: Everything You Need to Know to Become a Successful Building Service Contractor* (2nd ed.). Cincinnati, OH: Betterway Books, 1991.

Bewsey, Susan. *Start and Run a Home Cleaning Business* (2nd ed.). Bellingham, WA: Self-Counsel Press, 2002.

Lynn, Jacquelyn. *Start Your Own Cleaning Service: Your Step-by-Step Guide to Success.* Irvine, CA: Entrepreneur Press, 2003.

Becoming a Specialist

As you gain experience in your housecleaning business, you might find that particular aspects of the job intrigue you. You may be able to grow your business by specializing in areas you really love. Green cleaning—offering nontoxic, eco-friendly cleaning products and services—is the wave of the future; this can be

Throughout this book, we've met housecleaners across the country who are making a living and a career from housecleaning. Each cleaner is different, each business is different, each story is different. Yet there are some thoughts and lessons that come up again and again. As you plan your own housecleaning career, take a moment to ponder some lessons from the cleaners out there in the trenches.

• **Share the work.** Every cleaner we spoke to either worked with at least one other person regularly, or had a stable of friendly faces they could call on in crunch time. Husbands and wives worked together; friends and business partners shared the duties; sisters tag-teamed their assignments; families pitched in when needed. Cleaning is a hard job, and running a cleaning business is even harder. Share the burdens—and the joys. It helps. A lot.

• **Prepare for scheduling challenges.** Clients will insist upon living as far apart from each other as they can—or at least it seems that way! The logistics of getting from one appointment to the next are difficult for all cleaners. Plan on spending some time learning schedule management, and think ahead of time about how you'll handle those scheduling disasters that arise.

• **Get a Web site.** Those cleaners who have a presence on the Internet typically get 90 to 95 percent of their customers from their site. Many say customers seek them out. It's not a requirement, and it seems most effective in larger cities where population is dense. But the Internet is such a great business tool, it's worth a thought no matter where you live.

• **Go green.** Many cleaners who can provide real expertise in healthy, environmentally friendly practices and products are experiencing huge success, even in an economic downtown. Chances are that green will be the standard someday soon; why not get in on the ground floor?

• **Prepare to work hard.** Very hard. Probably harder than you've ever worked in your life. The labor is physical—lifting, bending, stretching, walking, climbing, staying on your feet for hours at a time. It's also mental—planning your marketing, your training, your mission statement, your schedule, your future. It can also be spiritual and emotional as you work through the heartaches and thrills of getting your very own business off the ground. It's never-ending. If you don't have a strong work ethic, this isn't the industry for you.

• **Take pride—and joy—in your work.** Every cleaner we spoke to pointed to "a sense of accomplishment at the end of the day" as one of the greatest delights of their work. It is indeed a rare and precious thing to stop at the end of each job, looking out over the expanse of a clean, fresh, sweet-smelling home, and know that you've brought a little order to a chaotic world. Savor it. You will have earned it.

a selling point for your business, and clients will be willing to pay more for your work if they know they aren't harming the earth. Chapter 7 focuses entirely on this specialty, which is poised to become the industry standard. Or think about some other specialties:

- Caring for antique furnishings and textiles—or historic properties in general. All require the loving hands of an expert.
- Caring for hardwood floors—or other specialized materials such as marble.
- Cleaning for those with allergies, asthma, or other health issues.
- Working with real estate agents, apartment managers, or home stagers to clean properties currently on the market. You might also focus on the cleaning needs of those moving into, or out of, a home.
- Working with event planners to offer before- or after-party cleaning.
- Working with builders to give just-built new homes their first cleanup.
- Disaster restoration: perhaps working and networking with insurance companies.
- Working with elder-care agencies or caregivers. Sometimes a little help with the sweaty stuff—and a regular check-in—can extend an older person's independent life by years, or decades.
- Combining housecleaning services with house- or pet-sitting, dog walking, errand running, lawn care, gourmet cooking, car washing, gift buying, interior decorating—anything you and your clients can think up!

It's *your* business, and you can take it in whatever direction you like.

We hope this book has offered you some ideas, information, and inspiration as you start up your own home-based housecleaning business. You have a lot of very hard work ahead of you, but the process can be more rewarding than you ever imagined. We wish you the very best!

Appendix I: Checklist of Start-Up Requirements

You might not need all of these items right away, but it's a good idea to have them in mind as you start up your business.

- ❏ Business license
- ❏ Fictitious name registration
- ❏ Liability insurance
- ❏ Bonding insurance
- ❏ Computer and accessories
- ❏ Internet service provider
- ❏ Business telephone line
- ❏ Telephone and voice-mail system
- ❏ Desk or table
- ❏ Chair
- ❏ File cabinets
- ❏ Fireproof safe
- ❏ Basic office supplies
- ❏ Basic cleaning supplies
- ❏ Vacuum cleaner
- ❏ Newspaper advertising
- ❏ Business checking account
- ❏ Merchant account
- ❏ Graphic designer for logo

Appendix II: Resources

Where to Get Your Business Questions Answered

Small Business Administration (SBA)

(800) UASK-SBA (800-827-5722)

answerdesk@sba.gov

www.sba.gov

For local offices of the SBA, check in your phone book under "U.S. Government" or visit the Web site.

The SBA is a terrific resource for business owners and potential owners, and it's free. At offices (called Small Business Development Centers or Business Information Centers) across the country, you can sign up for free training programs; receive free one-on-one counseling on everything from applying for a business license to paying taxes; and receive free publications on all aspects of starting, expanding, and operating your business. (These publications can also be downloaded from the SBA's Web site.) There are special programs for women in business, for socially and economically disadvantaged businesses, for veterans, and much more. (Two of these programs that may be especially useful are listed below.) Live online chats on all topics entrepreneurial—especially dealing with a slowing economy—are offered monthly. You can also find financial assistance in the form of individual counseling, loan application walk-throughs, and loan guaranties and disaster assistance. Did we mention that it's free?

Service Corps of Retired Executives (SCORE)

www.score.org (or contact your local office of the SBA)

SCORE, a resource partner with the SBA, is an all-volunteer nonprofit organization dedicated solely to helping small businesses succeed. Retired executives and business owners from all walks of life offer their knowledge as a community service. These folks know what they're doing, and they're dedicated to helping you. You can receive e-mail counseling or one-on-one counseling through local offices, or sign up for workshops and training. SCORE's Web site is also full of helpful information and links to every business resource you can imagine.

Office of Women's Business Ownership
owbo@sba.gov
www.onlinewbc.gov
Women business owners often face unique issues, and this organization can help you navigate your way through them all. You'll find workshops, roundtables, and one-on-one counseling opportunities to help you open, license, finance, and expand your business. The Online Women's Business Center Web site is helpful and inspiring.

Internal Revenue Service
(800) 829-1040 (for information or tax questions)
(877) 777-4778 (to reach the Taxpayer Advocate service)
www.irs.gov (click on "Businesses," then "Small Bus/Self-Employed")
Yes, we know, the idea of contacting the IRS *voluntarily* is a little intimidating. It can be done, and in fact the IRS has made good on its pledges to become a "kinder, gentler" organization. The Web site is a good place to start. You can download any form you might ever need, as well as dozens of publications. In particular, you might want to check out:

- Publication 583, Starting a Business and Keeping Records (includes sample forms)
- Publication 587, Business Use of Your Home
- Publication 910, Guide to Free Tax Services
- Publication 1546, The Taxpayer Advocate Service of the IRS

You can also request these by mail or phone.

Where to Get Your Housecleaning Questions Answered

The Internet

The World Wide Web offers a stunning amount of information on cleaning. Take advantage of others' knowledge and experience by typing "cleaning tips" or "house-cleaning" into a search engine. You'll have hundreds of thousands of sites to choose from, with everything from cleaning products for sale to enormous lists of tips for cleaning things you never even realized needed cleaning (bowling balls?). Many sites also offer e-mail connections so that you can contact the experts with your housecleaning questions. Some provide hotlines you can call when you're stumped. There are also newsgroups and forums where you can search other people's cleaning ideas, add your own, and discuss cleaning issues online. Do take everything on the Net with a grain of salt, however. You'll find fantastic advice, but you'll also find information from questionable sources, along with come-ons, scams, and brazen product hawking.

Books

There are a lot of good books on the market with all sorts of housecleaning tips—everything from removing stains to improving efficiency. Most of these are geared toward helping people clean their own homes, but you can tweak the information to suit your own needs. Here's just a small sampling:

Aslett, Don. *The Cleaning Encyclopedia: Your A to Z Illustrated Guide to Cleaning Like the Pros.* New York: Dell Publishing, 1993.

Bredenberg, Jeff, ed. *Clean It Fast, Clean It Right: The Ultimate Guide to Making Absolutely Everything You Own Sparkle and Shine.* Emmaus, PA: Rodale Press, 1998.

Editors of Consumer Reports. *How to Clean and Care for Practically Anything: Hundreds of Timesaving Solutions for All Around the House.* Yonkers, NY: Consumers Union, 2002.

All three of these books offer alphabetical listings describing how to clean just about every item or stain you can imagine, along with information about cleaning supplies and equipment. If you're ever presented with a thorny cleaning question (and clients will ask you about everything, from how to clean acoustical tile to how to remove chipmunk blood from velvet), these books can help you cope like the expert you are. All make for livelier reading than you might expect.

Campbell, Jeff, and the Clean Team. *Speed Cleaning* (3rd ed.). New York: Dell Publishing, 1991.

Jeff Campbell and the Clean Team (a California-based housecleaning service) offer a complete line of housecleaning resources, including several other books, a cleaning-products catalog, a Web site (www.thecleanteam.com), and even a hotline you can call with cleaning questions (800-717-2532, or click on the site's "Cleaning FAQ" to send your query to the team electronically). *Speed Cleaning* outlines a detailed method for cleaning houses as efficiently as possible. Whether you adapt all of the Clean Team's program or not, the book has some fine tips, especially on time management and environmentally friendly cleaning.

For books and other resources on eco-friendly green cleaning, see chapter 7.

Green Housecleaning

See page 100 for a list of some of the resources available on eco-friendly cleaning.

Support and Sanity for Entrepreneurs

Check out any of the following organizations, magazines, and Web sites to find whole communities of folks doing the same things you are: juggling self-employment with life, spouses, children, and mental health.

American Business Women's Association (ABWA)

9100 Ward Parkway
Kansas City, MO 64114
(800) 228-0007
www.abwa.org
Membership in ABWA entitles you to member discounts as well as education and support.

The Entrepreneurial Parent

(203) 457-9102
www.en-parent.com
A membership organization that offers advice, resources, newsletters, articles, and a community of self-employed parents. The Web site is worth checking out.

Home-Based Working Moms

www.hbwm.com

A professional association and online community.

Working Moms Refuge

www.momsrefuge.com

Advice, support, and discussions for working mothers—and working fathers.

Working Mother Magazine

www.workingmother.com

Appendix III: Blank Room Plans

One of the most important things you can do for yourself as you embark on your housecleaning career is to come to a clear understanding with your clients about exactly what services you will perform. Put this understanding in writing before you dust a single countertop! You and your clients will then know exactly what to expect. The room plans that follow are designed to help you get started with this kind of planning. Bring them along on consultations or use them as models to create room plans of your own, adapting them to fit your needs.

Client: _____ **Room: Vestibule**

Floor Finish

Wood _____ Carpet _____ Tile _____
Other _____

Wall Finish

Wood paneling ___ Tile ___ Paint over plaster ___ Washable wallpaper over plaster ___ Wood wainscoting ___ Plastic wainscoting ___ Other _____

_____

Entrance Door Wood ___ Metal ___ Door windows ___

Miscellaneous Tasks _____

_____

_____

_____

ETT: _____ minutes (Vestibule)

Client: _____ **Room: Living Room**

Floor Finish

Wood _____ Carpet _____ Tile _____
Other _____

Wall Finish

Wood paneling ___ Tile ___ Paint over plaster ___ Washable wallpaper over
plaster ___ Wood wainscoting ___ Plastic wainscoting ___ Other _____
_____

Appliances

Television ___ VCR/DVD ___ Stereo component unit ___ Humidifier _____
Other_____
_____
_____

Other Furnishings

Coffee table ___ Bookcase ___ End table ___ Paintings ___ Floor lamps ___
Table lamps ___ Miscellaneous _____
_____

Miscellaneous Tasks _____

_____
_____
_____

ETT: _____ **minutes (Living Room)**

Client: _____ **Room: Dining Room**

Floor Finish

Wood _____ Carpet _____ Tile _____

Other _____

Wall Finish

Wood paneling ___ Tile ___ Paint over plaster ___ Washable wallpaper

over plaster ___ Wood wainscoting ___ Plastic wainscoting ___

Other _____

Table

Wood ___ Glass ___ Acrylic ___ Other _____

Chairs

Wood ___ Upholstered ___ Other _____

Other Furnishings

Buffet _____

Breakfront Bar _____

Light fixtures _____

Paintings _____

Miscellaneous _____

Miscellaneous Tasks _____

_____

_____

_____

ETT: _____ minutes (Dining Room)

Client: _____ **Room: Family Room**

Floor Finish

Wood _____ Carpet _____ Tile _____
Other _____

Wall Finish

Wood paneling ___ Tile ___ Paint over plaster ___ Washable wallpaper over plaster ___ Wood wainscoting ___ Plastic wainscoting ___ Other _____

_____

Appliances

Television ___ VCR/DVD ___ Stereo component unit ___ Humidifier ___
Other _____ _____

_____

_____

Other Furnishings

Coffee table ___ Bookcase ___ End table ___ Paintings ___ Floor lamps ___
Table lamps ___ Miscellaneous _____

_____

_____

Miscellaneous Tasks _____

_____

_____

_____

ETT: _____ minutes (Family Room)

Client: _____ **Room: Den**

Floor Finish

Wood _____ Carpet _____ Tile _____
Other _____

Wall Finish

Wood paneling ___ Tile ___ Paint over plaster ___ Washable wallpaper over
plaster ___ Wood wainscoting ___ Plastic wainscoting ___ Other _____

_____

Appliances

Television ___ VCR/DVD ___ Stereo component unit ___ Humidifier ___
Other _____

_____

Other Furnishings

Coffee table ___ Bookcase ___ End table ___ Paintings ___ Floor lamps ___
Table lamps ___ Miscellaneous _____

_____

Miscellaneous Tasks _____

_____

_____

_____

ETT: _____ minutes (Den)

Client: _____ **Room: Office**

Floor Finish

Wood _____ Carpet _____ Tile _____
Other _____

Wall Finish

Wood paneling ___ Tile ___ Paint over plaster ___ Washable wallpaper over plaster ___ Wood wainscoting ___ Plastic wainscoting ___ Other _____

_____

Appliances

Television ___ VCR/DVD ___ Stereo component unit ___ Humidifier ___
Other _____

_____

Other Furnishings

Desk ___ File cabinets ___ Coffee table ___ Bookcase ___ End table ___
Paintings ___ Floor lamps ___ Table lamps ___ Miscellaneous _____

_____

_____

_____

Miscellaneous Tasks _____

_____

_____

_____

ETT: _____ **minutes (Office)**

Client: _____ **Room: Stairway**

Floor Finish

Wood _____ Carpet _____ Tile _____
Other _____

Wall Finish

Wood paneling ___ Tile ___ Paint over plaster ___ Washable wallpaper over
plaster ___ Wood wainscoting ___ Plastic wainscoting ___ Other _____
_____

Miscellaneous Tasks _____
_____
_____
_____

ETT: _____ minutes (Stairway)

Client: _____ **Room: Kitchen**

Floor Finish

Wood _____ Carpet _____ Tile _____

Other _____

Wall Finish

Wood paneling ___ Tile ___ Paint over plaster ___ Washable wallpaper over plaster ___ Wood wainscoting ___ Plastic wainscoting ___ Other _____

_____

Countertop

Wood ___ Fiberglass ___ Tile ___ Other _____

Sink

Porcelain ___ Acrylic ___ Stainless steel ___ Other _____

Appliances

Stove ___ Garbage disposal ___ Dishwasher ___ Refrigerator ___ Trash compactor ___ Microwave oven ___ Toaster oven ___ Other _____

_____

Miscellaneous Tasks _____

_____

_____

_____

ETT: _____ minutes (Kitchen)

Client: _____ **Room: Bathroom**

Floor

Laminate _____ Tile _____ Marble _____
Other _____

Tub/Shower

Fiberglass _____ Porcelain ____ Ceramic tile _____
Other _____

Toilet _____

Walls

Wooden wainscoting ___ Painted plaster ___ Tile ___
Other _____

Vanity

Porcelain ___ Stainless steel ___ Acrylic ___ Formica ___ Wood ___ Glass ___
Chrome ___ Other _____

Door

Wood ___ Glass ___ Other _____

Towel Rack and Wall Decorations

Chrome ___ Wood ___ Acrylic ___ Glass ___ Other _____

Miscellaneous Tasks _____

_____

_____

_____

ETT: _____ **minutes (Bathroom)**

Client: _____ **Room: Bedroom**

Floor Finish

Wood _____ Carpet _____ Tile _____

Other _____

Nightstand and Dresser

Wood _____ Glass _____ Acrylic _____

Other _____

Other Furnishings _____

_____

_____

_____

Miscellaneous Tasks _____

_____

_____

_____

ETT: _____ **minutes (Bedroom)**

Client: _____ **Room: Laundry Room**

Floor

Cement _____ Wood _____ Carpet _____ Tile _____

Other _____

Metal Appliances

Washer ___ Dryer ___

Utility Sink

Acrylic ___ Stainless steel ___

Other _____

Miscellaneous Tasks _____

_____

_____

ETT: _____ minutes (Laundry Room)